Deliverance from Error & Mystical Union with the Almighty

Al-Munqidh min Al-Dalal

Imam Ghazali

Translation & Introduction by
Dr Professor Muhammad Abulaylah, Al Azhar University

Dar Ul Thaqafah

Dar Ul Thaqafah

www.facebook.com/darulthaqafah
m.me/darulthaqafah
www.twitter.com/darulthaqafah

2023 CE – 1444 H

Translation of the Qur'ān

It should be perfectly clear that the Qur'ān is only authentic in its original language, Arabic. Since perfect translation of the Qur'ān is impossible, we have used the translation of the meaning of the Qur'ān throughout the book, as the result is only a crude meaning of the Arabic text.

Qur'ānic verses appear in speech marks proceeded by a reference to the Surah and verse number. Sayings (*Hadith*) of Prophet Muhammad ρ appear in inverted commas along with reference to the Hadith Book and its Reporter.

Contents

ABBREVIATIONS

AGth: G. Anawati and L. Gardet, *Introduction à la Thèologie Musulmane* (Paris: Vrin, 1948).

BM: M.C. Barbier de Meynard, "Traduction Nouvelle du Traité de Ghazzālī intitulé Le Préservatif de l'Erreur et Notices sur les Extases (des Soufis)," *Journal Asiatique* Series VII, vol. IX (1877), 5-93.

F: C. Field, *The Confessions of al-Ghazālī* (London: Wisdom of the East, 1909).

J: C.M. Jabre, *al-Munqidh min Aḍḍalāl* (Beyrouth, 1959).

Ja: C.M. Jabre, Arabic text of al-Ghazālī, al-Munqidh min aḍālal (see above).

M: D.B. MacDonald, "Emotional Religion in Islam as Affected by Music and Singing. Being a Translation of a book of the *Ihyā' 'Ulūm ad-Din* of al-Ghazzālī with Analysis, Annotation and Appendices. Bk XVIII" *Journal of the Royal Asiatic Society* (1901, pp. 195-252, 705-748; 1902, 1-28); "The Life of al-Ghazālī, with Special Refer ence to His Religious Experiences and Opinions," *Journal of the American Oriental Society*, XX (1899), 71-132.

Sch: A. Wensinck, *La pensée de Ghazzālī* (Paris, 1940).

VDB: S. Van den Bergh, *Averroes Tahāfut al Tahāfut* (London: Luzac, 1969).

VR: Laúra Veccia Vagliere and Robert Rubinacci, *Scritti scelti di al-Ghazālī* (Torino: Unione Tipografico-Editrici Torinese, 1970).

W: J. Watt, "The Authenticity of Works Attributed to al-Ghazālī," *JRAS* (1952), 26-27.

ACKNOWLEDGEMENTS

The Council for Research in Values and Philosophy (RVP) wishes to express its admiration for this work of Professor Muḥammad Abūlaylah and his wife, Dr. Nurshīf Abdul-Rahīm Rifʻat, both of al-Azhar University, Cairo, who together established this first critical Arabic edition. Professor M. Abūlaylah has produced an English translation marked by fidelity and clarity. This work is being published in a bilingual edition as well as separately in English and Arabic.

The participation of G. McLean in this project is due to the late Georges Anawati, O.P., and the Dominican Institute of Oriental Studies, Cairo, where the editor's introduction and notes and the editing of the English translation were realized.

The editor extends special acknowledgement to the late Richard J. McCarthy whose work, *Freedom and Fulfillment*, contributed substantively to the notes for the English translation and remains an excellent source of further information on the particular points.

Particular acknowledgement must be made also to The International Council for Philosophy and Humanistic Studies (CIPSH) and its parent organization UNESCO, Paris, for its support of this project.

TRANSLATOR'S INTRODUCTION

MUḤAMMAD ABŪLAYLAH

LIFE OF AL-GHAZĀLĪ

Al-Ghazālī's full name is Abū Ḥāmid Muḥammad Ibn Muḥammad Ibn Aḥmad al-Ṭusī al-Ghazālī (450-505 A.H./1058-1111 A.D.). In Latin his name was Algazel. He was known as The Proof and Ornament of Islam. He was an encyclopedic author, polymath, a great jurist, theorist, philosopher, theologian, moralist, critic, comparative religionist; above all he was a religious reformer and spiritual revivalist who sacrificed himself completely to his belief and ideal.

He was born in Ṭūs near Mashhid in Khurāsān in Persia. Having gained an excellent reputation as a scholar, he was appointed in 484 A.H. (1091 A.D.) by the Seljuk minister Niẓām al-Mulk to teach at Niẓāmiyya Academy founded by Niẓām al-Mulk in Baghdad. In this great city, al-Ghazālī's followers grew in number until they outnumbered even the retinues of the emirs and magnates (al-Safadī, *al-Wāfī bi al-Wafayāt*, ed. by H. Ritter et al. [Wiesbaden, 1962], pp. 274-277). Al-Ghazālī proved a great and influential lecturer in that institute. But in the month of Dhu'l Qi'da in the year 488 A.H. (1095 A.D.) after enduring a personal crisis he gave up the entirety of his worldly position and followed the path of renunciation and solitude. He performed the pilgrimage, and, upon his return visited Syria and lived there for some time in the city of Damascus. Thereafter he visited Jerusalem passing his time in worship, learning, contemplation and writing. After a life filled with great intellectual and spiritual achievements al-Ghazālī died on Monday, the fourteenth of Jumāda al-Ākhira in the year 505 (1111) at Tabaran, the citadel of Ṭūs, where he was interred.

Al-Ghazālī's writings, whether biographical or of general academic content, hold a faithful mirror to the society of his time and to his own person. From his writings we may glean not only details of his life, but also valuable information about his psychology and character.

Al-Ghazālī is not a merely theoretical writer. He illustrates his arguments with real examples, and his advice is based on his own experience. He was writing for people who were known to him and whose needs he knew very well. He was one of the greatest Imāms in the field of reformation, and as such he suffered from what we may call the sickness of his society and paid for it.

Great reformers have their sicknesses and sorrows, not because of their own state of health, but because the state of their nation drags them down and makes them feel ill. Their illnesses come from the social, moral and behavioral sicknesses of their society, from the sickbed of the nation, when it strays from the right path. Great people have suffered more from this kind of illness than from their own physical symptoms. Any physical sicknesses they had were slight compared with the sickness that came to them from contemplating their society.

The great man is a gift from God to his society, and a gift from God may be accepted or denied. Al-Ghazālī was both son and father to his society. He gave to it more than he took out. He continued his struggle against evil forces, ill-thinking, and false assumptions which traded on the name of Islam until death forced him to stop. He was not defeated by the persecution which his efforts brought upon him. He did not buckle under criticism; rather, it gave him added strength to stand his ground and to make his voice heard in all places and at all times.

If moralists had not been able to rouse themselves, they would not have been able to defend the higher ground of their convictions. The system of morals would have collapsed; virtue would have been buried alive; civilization would have become bankrupt.

Al-Ghazālī was "sick" from the people of his time. They were a trial to him. He was not a politician but he suffered the evils that afflict those who deal in politics. He was attacked by the germs of hypocrisy which surrounded his fellow scholars. He suffered because of the unhealthy differences which existed between Muslim sects, between Sunni and Shiite, which had reached a dangerous zenith in his day, and because of the corruption among the adherents of Sufism and the theologians.

In his time, the sects that claimed to be part of Islam were at war among themselves. Shi'a, Sunnī, Mu'tazila, Ismā'īlī, theologians, the patrons of the Brethren of Purity and the natural philosophers, all these, despite their differences, were ranged on one side, and al-Ghazālī on the other.

Knowing that al-Ghazālī suffered all his life from these major symptoms and maladies of his society, his own personal maladies seem slight in comparison. The great Imām was well aware of the link between his own poor health and the sickness of the society which besieged him.

As a child and as a young man before the age of twenty, he was recklessly ambitious and daring. He says that he thirsted after a comprehension of things as they really are. This was his obsession from an early age; it was instinctive, part of his God-given nature, a matter of temperament not of choice or contriving. But the more he progressed into the fields of the academic and religious thinking of his society, the more he suffered, to the point that at the time of his greatest success, when he occupied the highest academic chair in al-Niẓāmiyya University in Baghdad, teaching 300 students, he lost all desire to continue.

As has been mentioned before, al-Ghazālī writes about himself, his society, his religion and his Sufi experience. His writings shed light on each aspect of his time and display even the trivial details of history and the social disparities. In his voluminous encyclopedic work "The Revival of the Religious Sciences" he wrote about the religious branches of knowledge and the religious communities of his day. We have translated the *Book of Knowledge*, which is the first book of this work and provided it with an introduction.

Al Munqidh min al-Ḍalāl "The Deliverance from Error" may be categorized as autobiographical in nature. In this book, al-Ghazālī profiles some highly important information about himself as a man and as a thinker, and about his evaluation of contemporary religious thinking and trends. For this reason the book is of prime importance. We shall have the opportunity to discuss it later.

In his book *Bidāyat al hidāya* (*The Beginning of Guidance*) also, al-Ghazālī includes information about himself and the academic community of his time. Al-Ghazālī observed how people received his book, *Iḥyā'*, and he replied to criticism of it. He wrote a book about the different kinds of boasters, dividing them into groups, discussing and analyzing each in his own way. He wrote *Mi'yār al 'Ilm* (*The Yardstick of Knowledge*) to help confused students and academics perceive what knowledge is false, what is genuine: what should be accepted, what should be rejected. This led the Imām to write *Mizān Al-'amal* (*The Yardstick of Action*) and *Tahāfut al*

Falāsifah (*Contradictions among the Philosophers*).

We have listed these titles not in order to show how many books al-Ghazālī wrote, but rather to show how each volume was intended to deal with a problem and with problem-makers of his time.

Although Imām al-Ghazālī lived in difficult times we should not overlook the fact that this gave rise to his greatness. If his time was one of political upheaval and internal dispute in religion and sectarian factions, it was also a time of great scholars, and a time when knowledge was honored and learned men were respected and well paid. It was a time when a few chosen scholars could silence the hypocritical masses and purveyors of falsehood.

Al-Munqidh min al-Dalāl reflects al-Ghazālī's life and his own spiritual experience and development. There is no doubt at all about its authorship, but some critics have argued against its value as a historical document, as we shall see later.

Al-Ghazālī took issue with the scholars of the Bāṭiniyya sect, criticizing their principles and doctrines. He wrote several books about them and referred to some of them in the book translated here. This should add to his credibility as a sign of his courage in facing up to such dangerous opponents. We should keep this in mind when we turn to al-Ghazālī's political stance, which some critics have not taken into account. Defence of religion means defense of the state and of society as a whole.

From the title and introduction we can draw further insights. Al-Ghazālī was familiar with the causes of the confusion and errors that had befallen the nation. He says that most of the mistakes of the thinkers of his day came from believing what they had heard and were familiar with from childhood, having received it from their fathers, teachers and people regarded as virtuous. Al-Ghazālī had come to doubt what he had been told, and he urges others to doubt, as the reader of the present work will find.

He says that "anyone who does not doubt will not investigate, and anyone who does not investigate cannot see, and anyone who does not see will remain in blindness and error." Al-Ghazālī, here as elsewhere, considers skepticism as a source of knowledge and discovery because anybody who blindly accepts is not investigating or fathoming what he accepts. As a matter of fact, the Qur'ān urged people to doubt their father's beliefs, traditions and customs. Many verses of the Qur'ān say that Allah, referring to Himself, asks people if they have any doubts about His creations. This means that Allah expects people to doubt. Doubt can lead to a firmer belief, unless it is a symptom of a mental illness or spiritual disturbance. Faith in Allah can be deeply seated in the heart, but the heart still requires psychological reassurance, as in the case of Abrahām when he asked Allah how he could give life to the dead. Allah told him, "Don't you believe?" "Yes indeed I believe, but my heart needs to be at peace." This gnostic method, featured later in the work of Descartes, in fact is central to Descartes's philosophy.

Al-Ghazālī occupies a unique position among Islamic philosophers in recommending doubt within the boundary of faith. He was original and pioneering.

As we have already said, some critics have argued about the historical value of the *Deliverance from Error*. Some went as far as to say that it was intended as a novel, with himself as the central figure of the novel, a *Bildungsroman* (a development novel) as the Germans call this genre. These critics regard the book not as a true record of his real life and development, but as a fictional account written when he had finished developing. For example, 'Abdul Al-Dāim ál-Baqarī says that the *al-Munqidh* is neither an *Apologia pro vita sua* nor an autobiography, but a novel with a message, a sort of *roman a thèse*, with al-Ghazālī himself as the hero. He was trying to "leave to posterity a fictional image of his personality and create an interpretation of his life which would give him an unrivaled place in all the domains of thought and of the life of the Muslims of his time, including especially the knowledge and practice of *Taṣawwuf* (Sufism), with a dosage of avowals and insinuations which, without being totally false, would not correspond to historical reality." The crux of this argument is that al-Ghazālī himself said that his actions were not directed towards Allah, but towards his own quest for fame and prestige.

Al-Baqarī makes these avowals the explicative principle of the whole life of al-Ghazālī, his actions, movements, repose and intentions, not only before his withdrawal, but even after" (*I'tirāfāt al-Ghazālī*, Cairo, 1943; McCarthy, p. xxvi). This, in our view, is an untenable criticism. It stretches the text too far from its context and the author's psychology and career. Al-Ghazālī's confession should add to his reputation, rather than detract from it. Great people are never self-satisfied. Prophets look at their own work critically, unless it is revelation from God.

Once a phrenologist looked at a bust of Socrates and said, "This man is controlled by lust and imperfection." People responded vehemently that "this was the most virtuous man on earth." But Socrates said, "No, it is true. What he said is true about my nature, but I have striven to overcome the imperfections."

If al-Ghazālī told us about something in his inner self we should not take it as a means to attack him or to doubt what he says. In this case, we should look at the man's actions and his efforts to improve himself, not at his confession, nor should we hold that against him.

To doubt the reliability and historical value of al-Ghazālī's books, moreover, entails saying that al-Ghazālī was attempting in fictional form to prove the inferiority of the mind and the evidence of the sense compared with the illuminating light which Allah reveals to worthy men. This cannot be true when one sees al-Ghazālī's sincerity and devotion. The book itself cannot support this interpretation. In no way does it give the impression of being affectation. This is one reason, perhaps a psychological reason.

Secondly, all al-Ghazālī's other books and recorded conversations support what he says in this book, e.g., his conversation with the contemporary historian 'Abdul Al-Ghāfir al-Fārisī preserved by Ibn-'Asākir in his book *Tabyeen Kadhib al-Muftarī* as referred to in my introduction to the Arabic text.

Indeed, as a writer, the art of writing may cause one to shift emphases in the presentation. But the book holds a faithful mirror to the natural development of al-Ghazālī's character and knowledge.

Here we may refer to two poems written by al-Ghazālī himself at the time of his spiritual and intellectual doubts.

With light the face of Your Majesty was revealed.
And I wondered
and in You all manifest, lay my confusion.
O You are the nearest of things.
You have revealed Yourself, filling my view.
With Your manifestation of light, but becoming hidden
in a way which nearly left me without faith.
When You hid Yourself You threw between mind

and senses a difference that brooks no compromise.
If mind claims to know Your Presence and denies the
sense, who called it impossible.
The senses say to the mind stop here.
This is because the senses deny You O God as a
picture to be seen and the mind sees You through
*   abstract evidence*

Indeed I am so busy with the cultivation of my soul
and my business helps me to control myself.
The doubt of transitory things has been cast away from me
by a witness that comes like a beacon to me.
By it I have seen the Godly light very clear
from behind delicate screens that cover things,
then I became certain about the things
that previously I doubted.
And I have seen what was secret and hidden [to me]
And I have known the aim of my creation, the reason for
*   my existence.*
My death and my resurrection
by the mirror of the soul in whose bright surface there
*   appeared*
this world and the hereafter, the whole truth, the every aspect
*   of the truth.*
I know that no shade of doubt remained with me about
*   the things*
that make some people very doubtful.
The soul took its travelling staff and became sure that
*   my light had*
shone on the right road for me . . .
My light had shone over the face of my resting place as
evidence of what I have said.
There is the state of sleep, when the senses slip away while
*   you rest,*
and the tablet of the unseen faces the soul like two bright
*   mirrors,*
and what the tablet contains is reflected into the soul.

Then my soul takes its knowledge from there,
and the knowledge that I have is a copy of what is there.

This example can of course be multiplied. Al-Ghazālī was quite aware of his greatness, and we cannot take this as false self-importance.

He did show signs of arrogance and boastfulness, especially in his youth. Here and there he mentions something concerning his personality and experiences, not only in writing but also in conversation as referred to above. Moreover the earliest of his biographers, 'Abdul Al-Ghāfīr al-Fārisī (d. 529 A.H./1134 A.D.) wrote the following statement eighteen years after al-Ghazālī's death.

> He related to us on certain nights what his circumstances had been from the time he first openly followed the path of godliness and the mystical experience overcame him after he delved deeply into the various branches of knowledge and that he had behaved arrogantly to everybody, when he spoke boasting of how God's favor had singled him out, enabling him to master many kinds of knowledge and research them.
>
> He continued in this way until he felt disgust with the Arabic sciences which were not concerned with the hereafter and final goal, and what benefits and helps in the hereafter.
>
> He had begun his asceticism under the guidance and companionship of al-Farmadhī. From him he learned how to open up the gates to Sufism and followed his instructions about the performance of the duties of worship, of extra night-prayers, and of continual invocation of God's name — *Tariqa.*
>
> He continued in this way until he had overcome all these obstacles. He took on these burdens, but he did not achieve what he wanted. Then he related that he had studied every branch of knowledge and delved deeply into all aspects of learning and experience, and had again put all his strength and made every effort to study every complicated part of the sciences.
>
> He proceeded to the interpretation of these works

and continued to do so until he had unlocked the doors to every branch of knowledge.

He also told us that he became for a certain time busy with the counterbalancing of the proofs *Takafu' al Adilla* and the minute details of the problems. Then he told us that a door of the fear of God opened before him and took all his attention, forcing him to abandon everything else, until it became easy for him to accept the other way of religious practice. He then became perfectly disciplined and the reality of things became clear to him, and he turned into what we expected of him, behaving well with a good character and exact insight. This was the sign of the happiness which God had allocated to him before time began.

Then we asked him about how he had wished to leave his home and return to resume what was required of him in Nishabour (to teach in al-Niẓāmiyyah Academy). He said apologetically, "There was no way that my religion would permit me to refuse a request to spread God's message for the benefit of students, and indeed it was my duty to reveal the truth and speak about it and call others to it."

Later he abandoned teaching and returned to his home. He built a school beside his house where he could receive seekers after knowledge and provide a hostel for Sufis. Thereafter he divided his time according to those who would come to him, sometimes reciting the Qur'ān, sometimes sitting with the Sufis, sometimes teaching, so he did not waste a single moment of his time nor of other people's time.

In his late years al-Ghazālī occupied himself with the study of *Hadīth*, especially Al-Bukhārī's and Muslim's *Ṣaḥīḥs*. Shortly before his death, al-Ghazālī was reading in the *Ṣaḥīḥ* of al-Bukhārī, and it was reported that he died while the book was still in his hand. Al-Fārisī, adding to the statement above, mentioned that, "had al-Ghazālī lived longer he would even have ranked higher than the most eminent in the [Muslim] tradition." The following are some of 'Abdul Al-Ghafīr's statements about al-Ghazālī, not necessarily in the order in which they occur (Ibn 'Asakir, *Tabyeen Kadhib al-Muftari* [Beirut, Dār al-Kitāb al-'Arabī, 1979], pp. 291ff.): "He is a proof that Islam works as a system . . . the tongue of Islam . . . the Imam of the Imāms of religion . . . eyes have never seen another like him in his ability to speak, his eloquence, expression, quick understanding and natural command."

In Nishabour al-Ghazālī attended Imām al-Ḥaramayn al-Juwaynī's lectures and studied hard and graduated in a short time. He outstripped his fellows. He committed the Qur'ān to memory while still young and became the most able debater of his time and outstanding among the students of Imām al-Ḥaramayn. His fellow students benefitted from his teaching and guidance, and he never stopped learning. He began to write books. Imām al-Ḥaramayn, despite his high rank and his ability to talk fluently, did not regard al-Ghazālī with favor when they were alone together. This was because al-Ghazālī was quick to understand and his teacher was not happy that his student had started to compose books so early, although as his teacher it would reflect credit on him.

This is human nature, though the teacher appeared proud of al-Ghazālī in public and encouraged his success, but in his heart he nursed jealousy.

This situation persisted until Imām al-Ḥaramayn died in 478 A.H. (1085 A.D.). And then al-Ghazālī went to Nishabour and attended the assembly of the minister Nizām al-Mulk. The minister welcomed him because he ranked high as a scholar among the scholars and great Imāms who gathered at the minister's court.

Al-Ghazālī, no doubt, had benefited from this great assembly of rival scholars. His name rose over the horizon. Later al-Ghazālī moved to Baghdad to teach again in the academy during the ministry of Fakhr al-Mulk. Everybody there admired his teaching and skill in debating, and he did not find anyone his equal. After he had been the Imām of Khurāsān he became the Imām of Iraq. In this time al-Ghazālī wrote excellent books about *Fiqh* or Islamic Jurisprudence and its methodology. His fame now ranked higher in Baghdad so that it even outranked that of princes and officials of the caliphate administration.

But suddenly everything turned. He abandoned it all and gave up everything he suffered to attain in life and occupied himself wholly with religious duties and activities directed to the hereafter. He went to perform pilgrimage; then he went to Syria and remained there for ten years. While there he wrote such well-known and original writings as *Ihyā' 'Ulūm al-Dīn, The Revival of Religious Knowledge*.

He strove against his soul and his own behavior in order to perfect his own character and to cultivate his manner. Every bad quality in al-Ghazālī turned into a good one. He turned away from seeking fame and material gain and clothed himself in the garments of the righteous.

He scaled down his hopes in this world and devoted his time to guiding people to do what would benefit them in the hereafter, to make this world abhorrent to them, and to make them prepare for the long journey to the everlasting abode.

When he went back home, he busied himself with contemplation. He was visited by many people. He was a treasure supplying people's hearts with piety and guidance. His writings and books were widely disseminated and there was no contradiction between what he taught and how he lived.

No one objected to his teachings, and when Fakhr al-Mulk became a minister and heard of al-Ghazālī and admired his extensive knowledge, virtuous character, pure faith and sociability, he sought blessings from him, attended his classes and listened to his lectures. Then he asked him to return to teaching in the academy, so that his precious knowledge and fruitful learning should not be locked away without benefitting anyone. He begged him to accept his request and al-Ghazālī finally fulfilled his wishes and went to Nīshāpūr to teach in al-

Niẓāmiyyah.

The above summarizes the very important statement of 'Abdul Al-Ghāfir which has not been given enough attention by al-Ghazālī's modern biographers and critics. It is unfortunate that we cannot put a precise date for this conversation between al-Ghazālī and 'Abdul Al-Ghāfir. However it is possible to say that it occurred before al-Ghazālī finally withdrew from public life, and it is clear that no reference is made in this statement to al-Ghazālī's book *al-Munqidh* either as already written, nor did he mention any intention of writing it.

This is a definite indication that the book dates from later in al-Ghazālī's life. Even more importantly 'Abdul Al-Ghāfir asked him why he left his post in Baghdad and stopped teaching in the Niẓāmiyya. This is the precise question that appears at the beginning of *al-Munqidh*, and the whole conversation is more or less reproduced in the introduction of the book.

Al-Ghazālī tells us in the very first line of *al-Munqidh* that he wrote his book in response to a brother in the faith who had requested him to do so. We feel quite justified in saying that this brother in the faith was a real person, not a fiction or a literary device as McCarthy suggests, and not al-Ghazālī himself as 'Abdul al-Jalīl al-Baqarī assumed. We may even venture to assert that the brother in faith was 'Abdul Al-Ghāfir al-Fārisī himself or at least one of the people who attended the same meeting.

Al-Ghazālī and Public Life

Another line of criticism which is leveled against al-Ghazālī is that he did not take an active part in the wars between the crusaders and Muslims in his time. The army of the crusaders entered Antioch in Syria in 491 A.H. (1097 A.D.). 100,000 Muslims were killed in 495 A.H. (1101 A.D.). The Western forces captured Jerusalem and remained in control there for eleven years, but there is no mention of this in the writings of al-Ghazālī. This is strange when one bears in mind that he did mention dates close to these when speaking of his own career. He did speak about eminent figures such as Ibn Ḥanbal, Ibn Ḥazm, Ibn Taymiyyah, who were prominent in the struggle against political decay and corruption among the caliphs. I do not personally agree with the critics who accuse al-Ghazālī of ignoring political events. He did care about the Muslim nation, its religious stand and political supremacy. It is absurd to say that al-Ghazālī welcomed the invasion of Syria or felt happy about the mass killing of Muslims; it would be naive to think this.

A great personality can be perfect in one or more areas of life or of knowledge. This is true of al-Ghazālī's personality when it is examined closely. His character blossomed in the fields of scholarship, religion and social reform, particularly education. He was effective in restating the intellectual and spiritual basis of his time. He stood firm against the eminent representatives of the various sects and the authorities of his time (especially the Bātinites, who threatened the lives of their opponents with violence and assassination). In support of this point it is useful to refer to 'Abdul al-Qahir al-Baghdādī (d. 429 A.H./1037 A.D.) who said that in his time the Bātinites presented the most evil force and dangerous threat to Islam and Muslims ('Uṣūl al-Dīn, pp. 329-331).

Al-Ghazālī was uncompromising in his attitude toward them. He wrote several books attacking the Bātinites. In turn, they must have attacked him and even threatened his life — his constant move from place to place may lend support to this. Bearing this in mind, such a man cannot be accused of cowardice or opting-out. Al-Ghazālī took issue with the scholars of his time, especially the corrupt ones, emphasizing the importance of a good education for children since they are the basis and the new force of society. A society can be made strong through its children. Neglect of their education leads to a hypocritical, careless, faithless and loose generation of adults, corrupt rulers and cowardly army officers.

The author under review seems to have concentrated his attention on the source of corruption and decay in society, rather than upon the symptoms.

Al-Ghazālī had a good relationship with the rulers of his time but did not hesitate to advise them when he saw fit. It should be noted, however, that as a Sufi he criticized the scholars for consorting with rulers, but cannot be criticized for doing this very thing due to his integrity and drawing no advantage from their company. He lived a hard life until his death and never accepted the gifts of money that were offered. Rulers have to be supported, advised and corrected. They must not be left without scholarly and religious guidance, lest their views become narrow and they be surrounded by hypocrites and faithless opportunitists. Reforming the society, correcting the rulers and defending the people's human rights are the responsibility of the scholars and learned men. (See al-Subkī, *Tabaqāt*, vol. 4, p. 110. Also F.R.C. Bagley, *al-Ghazālī's* Book of Council for Kings [London, 1964].)

Another trend of criticism leveled at al-Ghazālī is that he retreated from public life for eleven years, leaving his people without the benefit of his advice. He should not be blamed for this, for he was preparing himself for a greater role later. Prophets and scholars of higher repute withdrew from society for long periods. It is obvious that our great Imām was inclined by nature to keep his distance. He perceived that mixing with people brings trouble. In his book *Iḥyā'* he wrote about the privileges of seclusion.

According to al-Manāwī, al-Ghazālī says in a poem, "In mixing with people there is no benefit, and ignorance about the reality of things is not like a scholar. You who ignorantly criticize me for keeping away from people, my reason [for doing this] is engraved on my ring." When they read the inscription on his ring they found this verse, "For the most of them we did not find any commitment to principle. We find that most of them are faithless" (Qur'ān 7: 102).

INTELLECTUAL MILIEU

Following the intellectual climate vividly referred to by al-Ghazālī, one is much impressed to see that al-Ghazālī became a meteor in the galaxy of the greatest scholars and divines of his time.

To cite but a few examples of al-Ghazālī's great contemporaries:

1. Imām al-Ḥaramayn, Abū al-Ma'alī 'Abdul al-Malik al-Juwaynī (d. 478 A.H./1085 A.D.), the mentor who discovered the young genius in al-Ghazālī and is rightly his moral and scholarly patron, as well as of the Nīshāpūr Academy, established also by Niẓām al-Mulk, in addition to heading many other institutions of teaching.

2. Abū Isḥāq al-Shīrāzī (418 A.H./1027 A.D.) who also headed Niẓāmiyya academy at Baghdad.

3. 'Abdul al-Salām Ibn Yusuf al-Nīshāpūr, Ibn Yusuf al-Qazwini (d. 482 A.H./1089 A.D.), the head of the Mu'tazilite school, who wrote a commentary on the Qur'ān in seven hundred volumes.

4. Abū Turāb, the head and the *Mofti* of the Ash'arites in Nīshapūr (d. 492 A.H./1098 A.D.).

5. Abū Muhammad al-Misrī (d. 486 A.H./1093 A.D.).

6. Abū 'Alī 'Ibn Ahmad al-Wāqidī (d. 468 A.H./1075 A.D.).

7. Abū Bakr al-Bayhaqī (d. 458 A.H./1065 A.D.).

8. Abū 'Alī al-Husayn 'Ibn 'Abdul Allah, Ibn Sīnā, known in the West as Avicenna, the greatest of Muslim philosophers, (370-428 A.H./980-1037 A.D.), and his disciple Abū 'Abdul Allah al-Masumi about whom Ibn Sīnā says, "Al-Masumi is to me what Aristotle is to Plato."

9. Omar al-Khayyām, the Persian astronomer and poet already mentioned in the introduction.

On the Sufi side, al-Ghazalī was a contemporary and quite aware of the following great figures:

Abū 'Alī al-Daqqāq (d. 415 A.H./1024 A.D.).

'Abdul al-Rahmān al-Sulamī the Sufi Qur'ān interpreter, historian and chronicler.

Abū al-'Abbas al-Qassār.

Abū al-Qāsim al-Qushayrī, the author of the celebrated *Risala* (Epistle) on Sufism and the Sufis. It is worth noting that in his section on metaphysics the author of *al-Munqidh* made reference to only two of the most eminent Muslim philosophers: Abū Nasr al-Fārābī (d. 339 A.H./950 A.D.), usually called the second teacher after Aristotle, and Ibn Sīnā (Avicenna 370-428 A.H./980-1037).

Ibn Sīnā deserves special attention here, since he is al-Ghazālī's contemporary, and was singled out by him as a specimen for moral criticism when he pinpointed the will in which Ibn Sīna recorded his confession of drinking alcohol and his pledge that he would never take the draught unless as medicine.

It is evident that Ibn Sīna was fond of banquets, luxury and being entertained. He used to deliver his lectures at night time and at the end of his lectures ordered a banquet to be laid and music to be played for the pleasure of his guests and pupils. He used to drink to excess until his health began to deteriorate. As a cure he took a powerful medicine which broke down his health. When he felt that his death was imminent, he stopped drinking and repented and asked God's forgiveness. Like al-Ghazālī, Ibn Sīnā died in his middle years. Yet it should not be overlooked that he was brought within the precincts of the Islamic tradition. He memorized the Qur'ān when he was ten years of age. He mastered Islamic and Arabic literature by the time he reached sixteen and became well-known in the whole of the Islamic world both as a physician and as a philosopher.

It is to the credit of Ibn Sīnā that he did not succumb to adverse sectarian influences. He himself said that his father often read the epistles of the Brethren of Purity, *Rasāil Ikhwān al-Safa*, yet was not influenced by them in any notable way. This in itself was a great sign of the independent mind and free-thinking he envisaged at an early stage of his life. In the same way as al-Ghazali, Ibn Sīnā was noted for his consistency from the beginning to the end of his life. The weight and style of his books in old age — say in his fifties — are as powerful and effective as those he wrote in his youth.

The first topic that appears immediately after al-Ghazālī's introduction to the *al-Munqidh* is sophistry: which is more or less a system of learning that misleads pupils or followers. In this section:

- 1st, al-Ghazālī, in his search after certitude, was ushered into false views.
- 2nd, when he resorted to reason, he discovered no distinction between his experience and the dream world.
- 3rd, he reverted to the guidelines of reason.

Al-Ghazālī began his career with the study of theology, but theology failed to satisfy him. Its objectives were the protection of the *sunna*, tradition, and its defense against the deviations of the heretics; it did not serve his purpose, which was the search for truth.

But it is striking that he placed the speculative theologians, Mutakallimūn, at the top of his list. The reason, as far as we can understand, is that this group of thinkers predominated over the rest and attracted people's attention. As they exercised immense influence upon the society suffering from illusions, it was al-Ghazālī's role to disillusion them from their sophistic illusions.

The eminent Sunnite scholars attacked the speculative theology of al-Kalām and strongly warned Muslims against preoccupation with it as an undesirable innovation. Al-Ghazālī himself wrote in more detail about the Kalām in his book *al-Iḥyā'*. As an illustration, he says, "Tawḥīd" the Oneness of God is the term which has changed its meaning. It now means the craft of theology, knowledge of methods of arguing and confronting adversaries, boasting, multiplying questions, casting doubts on matters, and showing down opponents. This is true to the point that some practitioners, i.e, Mu'tazilites, called themselves the people of justice and pure monotheism.

In his search for truth, Imām al-Ghazālī turned to philosophy, including the natural sciences, which gave him a penetrating insight into the marvels of creation. In the view of al-Ghazālī no one who had studied anatomy could fail to notice the perfection of human and animal organs and to recognize in them evidence of the creator's master hand. He found himself unable to go along with the natural scientists, in particular he emphatically rejected their denial of resurrection and sensual pleasure and punishment in heaven. But it should be noted that he does not reject philosophy and science altogether, he still believed that there was much truth in Aristotle, who like Plato and Socrates was regarded as a "theist". The Imām sums up his view of the philosophers and scientists by pointing out that they served neither to prove nor disprove the existence of God. Al-Ghazālī urged that the majority of people should be protected from potentially harmful ideas: he refers to the Epistles of the Ikhwān al-Ṣafā and then says in warning, "Just as the poor swimmer must be kept from the slippery banks, so must mankind be kept from reading these books" and by analogy all similar books that can mislead and harm the average Muslims. After examining philosophy al-Ghazālī stepped out of it and continued his search for truth.

True knowledge is derived from divine inspiration (from faith, rather than from the dictates of dry logic). Out of this combination of guiding reason and inspiring and unflickering Faith in the Divine, al-Ghazālī emerged. From this station he became the triumphant exponent of the religion of Islam, and thus was fittingly called Ḥujjat ul Islām, the proof of Islam.

TRANSLATIONS AND EDITIONS OF *AL-MUNQIDH*

The text of *al-Munqidh* was discovered in 1842 A.D. by the scholar, Auguste Schmölders, who found the text, translated it into French and published it for the first time in Paris. Sixty-seven years later in 1909, the text appeared in English, translated by Claude Field under the title, *The Confessions of al-Ghazālī.* This translation reads well for the most part, but could be more faithful and precise. Professor Watt's translation tried to improve on Field's version. It was published under the title, *The Faith and Practice of al-Ghazālī* (London: George Allen & Unwin Ltd., 1953). We have already said something about this version. The third and most recent translation into English is by Richard Joseph McCarthy, S.J., and bears the title, *Freedom and Fulfillment* (Boston, 1980). The volume includes also related texts by al-Ghazālī translated by McCarthy. His translation reads well and is painstakingly clear and accurate. He benefited from previous translations and scholarly works on al-Ghazālī, drawing heavily on the studies by Poggi and Jabre. In his lengthy introduction of sixty pages (the text of the translation is fifty-three pages) and plentiful footnotes, McCarthy emphasizes the uniqueness of al-Ghazālī and the importance of studying his thought.

McCarthy based his translation not only on the well-known edition, but also on a new manuscript given to him by Father Poggi dated 509 A.H (1115-1116 A.D), i.e. five years after al-Ghazālī's death and about ten years after *al-Munqidh* was composed. However, McCarthy is fully aware that there is no serious difference between this early manuscript and the one used by Salībah and 'Ayyād, Jabre and Watt. In editing our critical Arabic text we have checked other manuscripts and several other editions of *al-Munqidh*.

McCarthy read the previous translations and decided that there was still a need for his new one. He tells us that his translation was written while he was reading *al-Munqidh* to his students at Oxford, when he came up with some ideas that he thought worth publishing. McCarthy believes that his translation reads better and gives a more fair reflection of al-Ghazālī's life than do previous versions.

Reading that translation and the footnotes, we may say that the translation is good, but still not perfect; it has not deterred us from our decision to make yet another translation. Beyond doubt, McCarthy has done justice to the text, illuminating its meaning and making it available to speakers of English. His footnotes, in general, serve the text well and enable us to understand al-Ghazālī's statements.

Nevertheless, on some occasions the footnotes are too bulky, incorporating irrelevant material, and addressing the general reader rather than the specialist. He refers to secondary sources and does not refer the *Hadīths* back to their respective authorities; in several cases he failed to identify al-Ghazālī's sources. McCarthy's translation of the *Hadīth* about the division of the Muslim nation into sects is incomplete and incorrect. Occasionally he confuses his reader when he refers to the authority of a certain *Hadīth*.

We therefore intend to introduce our own translation, feeling that it is needed and will prove useful. I will not try to justify this decision beyond saying that Allah directed me to produce this translation which is directed wholly and sincerely to Him.

Our translation takes into consideration the other translations in English, particularly M. Watt and McCarthy, and also the fragments of *al-Munqidh* that are in circulation in the writings of the orientalists.

We have noted some differences in understanding the text and we have differed also from Farid Jabre's French translation (Beirut, 1969), which appears in the bibliography. We have sought to give the most lucid rendering — one that we consider much closer to al-Ghazālī's text and trend of thought.

We have read and checked the available outstanding Arabic editions of this remarkable text. Two rare manuscripts: first, Shahīd Ali Pasha, no. 1712, Istanbul, which is complete and well-written, and which dates from 509 A.H.-510 A.H. (1115 A.D.-1116 A.D.), five years after the death of the author. The second one is Ṭal‘at, Cairo, Dār al-kutub, no. 637, which is important yet incomplete.

Two outstanding Arabic editions deserve special comment: The Arabic text first published in Damascus (1956) by Jamīl Ṣalībah and Kāmil ‘Ayyād is good in the main; it is not the first edition of *al-Munqidh* from the chronological point of view, but to a great extent it is the most readable and tolerable version. The authors based their edition on the available extant Arabic versions. As they remarked, it was only by chance that they struck upon a single manuscript which lends authenticity to the Arabic version on which we are working. It should be noted, however, that the manuscript they had in hand was recently copied from an unknown and unverified version.

But luckily enough the difference between the printed, published version, on the one hand, and the extant available manuscript, on the other hand, is not serious in many cases. Hence, our work and painstaking effort is to bring out a better, more critical and perfectly readable text. This can be seen from our Arabic version, found here, if read against other versions in circulation.

The second version to attract our critical attention is the version of *al-Munqidh* by his Eminence Sheikh Abdul Al-Halīm Maḥmoūd (Cairo, Dar-al Ma'arif, 1988). Sheikh Abdul Al-Halīm is a leading exponent of Sufism in modern times, and was known among his followers as the al-Ghazālī of Egypt. He was an eminent scholar, well respected in Egypt and worldwide. I am proud to have had him as my mentor and to have received his special attention while still an undergraduate at Al-Azhar University.

Notwithstanding his erudition and practical Sufism, when he took upon himself to publish a new version of the *al-Munqidh* he concentrated his attention on a long introduction explaining the theory of Sufism, rather than focusing on the textual evaluation of the prototype version. His introduction covers almost 320 pages in comparison to al-Ghazālī's original book which has only 80 pages, excluding the space given to the footnotes.

Al-Ghazālī's name did not appear on the cover and title pages. Its first mention is on p. 138, in the context of his "Fatwa" quoted in full by the editor. The second is on p. 214 in the context of his challenge to the principles of knowledge.

After the Sheikh's exhaustive explication of Sufism from its original sources to modern times, he devoted the fifth section of his introduction to al-Ghazālī and his milieu, pages 269-323. The information given about al-Ghazālī is based almost entirely on quotations and soon digresses from *al-Munqidh* to *Iḥyā' Ulūm al-Dīn* by the same author as an independent subsection occupying 33 pages. Nothing is said about the *al-Munqidh*.

It must be noted that there are editorial mistakes in Sheikh Abdul Al-Halīm's version, which still appear in its third edition (Cairo, Dār al-Ma'arif, 1988). Some editions of *al-Munqidh* have not escaped editorial mistakes/errata, yet are tolerably acceptable. To save time and energy, however, it is expedient to turn to the main point of the present work.

CONTENT AND VALUE OF
AL-MUNQIDH MIN AL-ḌALĀL

Al-Munqidh min al-Ḍalāl is not only the greatest, but the crown of all al-Ghazālī's work. It is small in size, but as a document is great in scholarly and historical value. It sheds light on al-Ghazālī's personality and provides unique details about his life, milieu and other related issues.

Al-Munqidh does not limit itself to one approach to its subject. It starts from one point and aims toward one goal, but explores many roads to this end. This book may be loosely categorized as autobiographical, although it was not intended to be an autobiography in the strict sense. Islamic literature did not include such a category in the way that it developed in the West. This may be because Islam forbids anyone to boast of his own achievements or to talk about himself. Some early biographical information is found in the philosophical and literary writings of Muslim scholars as indicated elsewhere in this introduction, but there is no class of autobiography as such. This may be the reason why al-Ghazālī did not give more information about himself in the book under focus. If he had not been bound by the conventions of his time, what fascinating details he could have given us.

The facts that he does give about his own life are impressive and are phrased in a masterly fashion and a highly developed spiritualism. They are scattered in many of his works. If assembled in one place they would be enjoyable and rewarding. For example, in *al-Munqidh* he spoke of Sufism as his last permanent home, and gave the reasons for preferring it above other systems. In other writings he describes how he virtually became a Sufi himself and took the Sufi way and developed his experience of Sufism.

Al-Munqidh has three major dimensions; first, the autobiographical dimension which is indispensable in understanding al-Ghazālī's works and milieu; secondly, the psychological and intellectual graph which records al-Ghazālī's inner experience, intellectual endurance and response to the power of the moment; and thirdly, an investigation of the religious and intellectual trends of the time and milieu, analyzing and rectifying them from his position as a philosopher and religious reformer.

Al-Ghazālī wrote *al-Munqidh min al-Dalāl* at the age of fifty. The precise date of this book is not noted, but is not impossible to identify. He wrote it between 499 A.H./1105 A.D.) and 500 A.H./1106 A.D., about five or six years before his death. This in itself indicates that al-Ghazālī was quite active up to the very end of his life.

So far as is known to scholarship, it is the last of his whole life's work. It is therefore not surprising that it encapsulates all aspects of his spiritual and intellectual experience and output. Therefore, it is full of re-capitulatory references epitomizing his major works. In essence, it is the flower and fruit of his journey in his short life span.

In 1842 *al-Munqidh* was discovered and first translated into French by Auguste Schmölders. The book itself bears two titles. The first is *Al-Munqidh min al-Dalāl wa al Mufṣiḥ 'an al-Aḥwāl.* (*The Deliverance from Error and the Revealer of the Mystical States of the Soul*). The second is *Al-Munqidh min al-Dalāl wa al-Muwaṣṣil ila Dhī al-'Izza wa al-Jalāl* (*The Deliverance from Error and the Deliverer to the Possessor of Power and Glory*).

There is good reason to believe that these titles were concurrent. In his book, *Ḥayy Ibn Yaqzān* (Cairo: Ṣubayḥ, 1978, p. 9), Ibn Ṭufayl (d. 581 A.H./1185 A.D.) refers to *al-Munqidh* under the first of the two long titles with an insignificant variant of the preposition — using *bi* in place of *ann*. The two different forms of the title both start with "Deliverance from Error", showing that al Ghazālī himself had experienced the confusion of being wrong, or rather had been part of a society in error. He was exploring the way to set his foot on the right path, looking for the kind of character which would choose the right path.

We may ask why al-Ghazālī chose to call his book "*Deliverance from Error*". The Prophet Muḥammad (Peace be upon him) says, "I have left two things for you. If you take hold of them you will never go astray. They are the book of Allah and my *sunna* (i.e. my example)." There is no doubt that al-Ghazālī knew this *Ḥadīth* and had strong faith in the Qur'ān and the *sunna*. Eminent scholars such as Aḥmad Ibn Ḥanbal and Abū al-Ḥasan al-Asha'rī had guided people along this path and had formulated the Muslim articles of faith. The phrase "deliverance from error" might be applied to their teaching; how, then, did al-Ghazālī choose it for his own book?

Al-Ghazālī certainly did not propose his book as a substitute for the Qur'ān and *Sunna*. Close reading of his book reveals that there is no true guidance outside the book of Allah and the life of the Prophet Muḥammad (Peace be upon him). But we should read his book in the context of the society of his time. Corruption was rampant, as were secular claims and theories, sectarian arguments, underground movements and false ideas dressed in Islamic clothing. Al-Ghazālī prepared to attack all these elements by approaching them in their own way, using their own methods. His aim was to set up a model and criteria for testing other theories. Titles of other books by him reflect this approach — they included "The criteria . . .", "The way to measure . . .", "The straight path . . ." and so on.

From al-Ghazālī's title and introduction we note that, first, he emphasizes that he lived in a time of error, his society was going astray, especially those who claimed to be scholars eminent in religious studies; his age was in urgent need of a savior to deliver them from error. This was perhaps the reason why al-Ghazālī wrote his book, to emphasize two points at one and the same time: his credibility as a person to lead the people from destruction to a pure life and a strong faith, and also to show the method of deliverance. Secondly, we note that al-Ghazālī explained spiritual and intellectual corruption and psychological maladies as resulting from ignorance and blind conformity. Thirdly, Muslim society at the time of al-Ghazālī was divided into many sects. The most persistent and damaging was the Bāṭiniyya teaching, which presented a threat to the Muslim Caliph and his officials. They aimed not merely to spread their doctrine, but to assassinate the major figures among their opponents. Niẓām al-Mulk and Fakhr al-Mulk, the ministers who were al-Ghazālī's patrons, were assassinated by them.

The book comprises an introduction and eight main topics. The addressee in al-Ghazālī's customary *khuṭba*, introduction, is not directly mentioned and some scholars think that it is properly a generic salutation. But close reading of data at our disposal gives the strong impression, if not a real clue or a clear allusion, that the addressees were either 'Abdu al-Fārisī his biographer (al-Subkī, *Ṭabaqāt al-Shafi'iyya*, Cairo, vol. 3, p. 137), or Abū Bakr Ibn al-'Arabī (d. 543 A.H./1148 A.D.), who evidently had met al-Ghazālī shortly before he embarked on the writing of *al-Munqidh (al-*

'Awāṣim min al-qawāṣim, Algeria, vol. 1, p. 30). A little-known fact about *al-Munqidh* is that al-Ghazālī states in his introduction that he wrote the work at the request of a brother in faith who asked him to reveal secrets of the sciences, and the dangerous depths of the schools of thought. What prevails with most scholars is that it was meant for a type of reader, and not for a particular individual. This vast majority, beating around the bush, has come nearer to the point but have fallen short of grasping it.

In brief, we can summarize al-Ghazālī's meaningful introduction in two cardinal points. First and foremost, from the earliest stage of his life, al-Ghazālī had been known as a fearless, sagacious, uncompromising seeker after truth. Secondly, al-Ghazālī's time was an epoch of vigorous intellectual activity and spiritual fecundity, so much so that for the average Muslim layman the controversies and sectarian cerebral confrontations resulted in little more than a welter of confusion and perplexities. For this very reason, *al Munqidh* offered itself as means of provoking intellectual initiative and enkindling spiritual intuition for the purpose of pronouncing sentence on faulty sects.

RENOWN

Through Western translations and scholarship on *al-Munqidh*, al-Ghazālī is well-known to the scholars and reformers as a magnanimous, indefatigable and inexhaustible source of inspiration and impetus in exploring the higher realm of learning and scholarship. Some of al-Ghazālī's works were translated into Latin in the Middle Ages, e.g., his books *Maqāsid al-Falāsifah* (*The Intentions [or Aims] of the Philosophers*) and *al-Iqtisād fil I'tiqād* (*The Golden Mean in Belief*), and later into several modern European languages. Hardly do we find a book on Islamic civilization without reference to al-Ghazālī. A good number of orientalists have produced several works of outstanding value on his life and milieu. Many others have dealt with al-Ghazālī within the scope of their writings and research. The output of the crop of orientalist writings on al-Ghazālī is so voluminous as to defy classification in our present work. Baron Caradivo, e.g., wrote a book on al-Ghazālī (trans. into Arabic by Zi'iater [Cairo: al Ḥalabī, 1950]) in which he explored the real position of the author of *al-Munqidh* in Ṣufī literature and practice.

He noted that "*al-Munqidh* is a great psychological document of al-Ghazālī's time . . . ."

D.B. Macdonald summed up the significance of al-Ghazālī and the pioneering role he played in Muslim thinking in four main points. First, he discarded empty abstract scholasticism and dogmas, and substituted direct contact with the Qur'ān and *Sunna* (tradition). Secondly, he laid emphasis on the fear of Allah by urging moral rectitude to avoid the punishment of hell. Thirdly, it was he more than any other that established Islam on a firm and assured ground. Fourthly, he brought philosophy and theology within the grasp of the ordinary mind. (See *Aspects of Islam* [New York: Books for Libraries Press, 1971], pp. 36, 139, 194, 196-201; also "The Life of al-Ghazālī", *JAOS* 20 [1899], pp. 70-133.) This statement sounds scholarly, but cannot pass without comment. Regarding the first point, it is absolutely correct that al-Ghazālī brought the message of the Qur'ān and *Sunna* to ordinary life in clearer insight and practicality, i.e., from the ivory tower of scholasticism to the tangible and palpable reality of religion. To establish this al-Ghazālī had to wrestle with exponents of sectarian thinking and speculative theologians and jurists.

Concerning MacDonald's second point it is worth noting that al-Ghazālī, through emphasizing the importance and effect of the fear of Allah, also emphasized, on the other hand, the importance of hope in salvation. In his own simile, "Hope and fear are like two wings by which one can fly and attain divine satisfaction and solace. They are like two mounts on which every steep ascent of the paths of the next world is traversed."

A deeper insight of al-Ghazālī's literature on fear is that the fear of the creator leads to an even greater hope in Him; hope alone, without fear, cannot lead to bliss and paradise. Fear is a natural propensity without which, man cannot attain his equilibrium.

Indeed, it is true that al-Ghazālī's analysis of fear is more elaborate than that of hope, and that he devoted a great deal of his book to it. This is partly because of his belief that fear had the greater relevance in the contemporary situation, but it is also accounted for by its place in al-Ghazālī's gnostic or mystical themes, and its importance for his theology of which predestination is the cornerstone. To our Imām fear is well connected with the knowledge of God: when knowledge of God is perfected, the majesty of fear and the conflagration of the heart are produced. Then the trace of conflagration rushes from the heart to the body and behavior (*ibid.*, p. 27). It is perhaps because of this mode of writing that Malise Ruthven sees in al-Ghazālī's writings a sense of sadness and seriousness; he says, "Al-Ghazālī's work lays down the role of an earnest, somewhat joyless religiosity, pregnant with *gravitas* and un-leavened by humor" (*Islam in the World* [London: Penguin Books, 1991], p. 241). To illustrate this, he refers to the following *Ḥadīth* cited by al-Ghazālī in his book *al-Iḥyā'*, "The man who speaks a word to make his friends laugh is thereby hurled into the pit of hell for seventy years."

In his book, *Islam*, (p. 94), H.A.R. Gibb, says that al-Ghazālī, "is a man who stands on a level with Augustine and Luther in religious insight and intellectual vigor." Yet in our view, he stands head and shoulders above them since he is more universal than restricting himself to one creed.

To Ignaz Goldziher al-Ghazālī, "is one of the most epoch-making personalities."

In his contribution to *Religion in the Middle East: Sufism*, Martin Lings holds al-Ghazālī as the most famous among those Sufis who had bridged the chasm between Sufism and the rest of the Islamic community. Lings says, "Al-Ghazālī . . . the great Shāfi'i canonist and theologian who devoted his latter years to mystic paths and who wrote an autobiographical treatise, *Deliverance from Error (al-Munqidh min al-Ḍalāl)*, in praise of Sufism as the only sure antidote to skepticism and as the highest way to life" (vol. II, p. 264).

To Montogomery Watt who has translated *al-Munqidh* together with *Bidāyat al hidāya* into English, "Al-Ghazālī is one of the great Muslim thinkers, though, perhaps over-esteemed in the West." The reason for Watt's statement that the Westerners find it easier to be sympathetic with him requires more explanation. Certainly, al-Ghazālī deserves to be loved and appeals to all who have a noble and fair mind. Watt himself nuanced his statement as appears in his article on al-Ghazālī in the new edition of the *Islamic Encyclopedia*.

Referring to the appeal of *al-Munqidh*, Watt stated that "this again is largely due to the charm of his *apologia pro vita sua*, entitled *Deliverance from Error*, which he completed two or three years before his death in December 1111. To fill out our understanding of the Islamic world up to 1100 it is well worth looking more closely at al-Ghazālī." In his work, *Deliverance from Error*, al-Ghazālī relates how, after a period of skepticism, he resolved to make an active search for ultimate (religious) truth among the rational theologians, the philosophers, the Bātinites (i.e., Ismāʿīlites) and the Sufis or mystics (*The Majesty That Was Islam* [London: Sidwick and Jackson, 1974], p. 252f).

Richard Joseph McCarthy who brought out another translation of *al-Munqidh* considers *al-Munqidh* to be unique in the whole of classical Arabic and Islamic literature. But McCarthy doubts whether this outstanding book is the first of its kind. Al-Ghazālī's originality in *al Munqidh* is in the great tradition of Muslim autobiography or quasi-biographical literature. It is true that before al-Ghazālī, Ibn Ḥazm al-Andalusi wrote his *Ring of the Dove, Ṭūq al-Ḥamāma* and *al-Akhlāq wa Siyar*, in which he provided much autobiographical information. This can be taken in one way or another as internal evidence that al-Ghazālī was influenced by Ibn Ḥazm in this field. Ibn Sīnā, and al-Fārābī before al-Ghazālī both had written a large amount of autobiographical material. (Ibn Abī Uṣaybia's ʿUyūn al-Anbā', vol. 3, pp. 3-29 and 223-233.) It is to be noted that autobiography is not an independent Islamic genre or branch of knowledge.

He compares favorably the rhetoric and genre of al-Ghazālī in *al-Munqidh* with that of the English academic theologian and activist, John Henry Newman, of the nineteenth century Oxford movement. Though Frick more cautiously refers to it as an *apologia pro doctrina sua*, McCarthy still thinks that *al-Munqidh* possesses its own uniqueness for reasons which are self-evident and self-proclaimed.

McCarthy's own translation is accompanied by a long and useful introduction about al-Ghazālī and *al-Munqidh*, and with appendices and annotations. The introduction is sixty pages, the translation fifty-three pages, the annotations of twenty-eight pages, and the indispensable appendices stretch from p. 145 to p. 297 of the book containing a translation of other works by al-Ghazālī mentioned in the book.

McCarthy worked intensively with the Jabre and Poggi translations (e.g., vide p. xxlx) and utilized to a certain extent the available translations of *al-Munqidh*, including those in Dutch and Turkish. He specifically mentioned Field's and Watt's translations.

He based his translation on the Arabic text printed by Jamīl Salībah and Kāmil Ayyād, which was used also for Jabre's French translation and Watt's translation. Notwithstanding all this, he perused the Shahīd 'Alī Basha's manuscript dated 509 A.H. (1115-1116 A.D.) i.e. five years after al-Ghazālī's death, which we have also used in our translation, together with another good, yet incomplete manuscript (Taymūr, Bash, Egypt-National Library).

For the first time, we are introducing our edition of *al-Munqidh* in its Arabic original; the translation here is based on our own edition.

This translation, though not the first one, certainly is the first by a Muslim who stands very close to al-Ghazālī's personality and spirit. The translation, it is hoped, reads smoothly and carries much of al-Ghazālī's style, warmth and stamina in the sphere of learning and truth.

EDITOR'S INTRODUCTION

GEORGE F. McLEAN

THE CONTEXT

In order to understand a person's life it is usually helpful to know something of his or her social, political and cultural contexts. How important this is depends, on the one hand, upon theoretical considerations and, on the other hand, upon the person him or herself. The theoretical issue is the extent to which a person is understood in terms of interiority vis-à-vis in terms of openness and relation to others. Indeed, deep reflection suggests that the degree of one's interiority and reflective self-possession is the key to one's ability to relate to others with that free and passionate sense of justice which is the fruit of love.

This is important for a personal history. Without this balanced sense of the person, on the one hand, a life would be interpreted simply in terms of external events or powerful political authorities, in relation to whose concerns the individual is but a marionette. Worse still, any claim to personal and free decision making would be interpreted as fraud or deceit. On the other hand, that same life could be interpreted in a simply self-reflective manner, reducing it to egoistic self-seeking, missing its social concern and impact, and — even more — losing the significance of personal and religious interiority for the life of society as a whole.

All of this is especially true in the concrete case of al-Ghazālī who lived at the center of an intensely religious culture, the understanding and development of which was his central concern and major accomplishment. D.B. MacDonald described him as "the greatest, certainly the most sympathetic figure in the history of Islam," the only teacher which later generations of Muslims ever put on a level with the four great Imāms. For W.M. Watt "al-Ghazālī has sometimes been acclaimed in both East and West as the greatest Muslim after Muḥammad, and he is by no means unworthy of that dignity."[1]

To see the socio-political, indeed the geo-cultural, context in its true perspective it is helpful to take up the suggestion of Marshal G. Hodgson, at the beginning of his *The Venture of Islam: Con-*

science and History in a World Civilization.[2] He argues effectively that to understand not only Islam, but world civilization it is necessary to break free from Eurocentrism. In the Middle Ages the central drama of world civilization was not being played out in the small kingdoms of Western and Southern Europe. Rather it consisted in the emergence of Islam in confrontation with Byzantium to the East, from the Nile to the Oxus, where the Irano-Semitic culture is found. In this context, the Roman Empire and Western Christianity shrink in relation to the importance of the emergence of Islam to the East.

Prior to al-Ghazālī Islam had undergone an explosive development. In the century after the life of the Prophet Muḥammad (570-632 A.D.), it expanded with remarkable swiftness across Africa to Spain in the West and far to the East. The unity of religious and social authority in Muḥammad and in the Islamic community faced heavy challenges during the second century of Islam when the spiritual authority of the Caliph was submerged by the military, and hence political, power of the Sulṭāns. The early orthodox Caliphate of ʿUthmān and others was succeeded by the Umayyad caliphate and this, in turn, by the ʿAbbasid caliphate. It was during the later, declining period of this caliphate that al-Ghazālī lived (1058-1111 A.D., or the years 450-505 A.H. counting from Muḥammad's Hegira or trek from Macca to Medina).

The guard of the Abbasid Caliphs, which was drawn from foreign, especially Turkish, elements assumed the real political power. They were replaced by the Persian Buwayhid from 945-1055, who were replaced in turn for a century by the Turkish Seljukides, when Caliph al-Qā'im recognized Toghrul Beg as Sulṭān in Baghdad. This began a line which for a century would rule the vast expanse from the Mediterranean to Afghanistan.

During this time, which was that of al-Ghazālī, a strong attempt was underway by the Fatimides of Egypt to supplant the sunnite Abbasid Caliphs in order to assume the religious and political leadership of all Islam. Claiming to be descendents of Ali, successor of Muḥammad, and Fatima, his daughter, they brought together the Shīʿite Alides and conquered North Africa, where Cairo became their capital. Their intent was to dominate Iraq, Syria, Khorasan and the entire Abbasid empire. To this end Ḥassan b. Sabbāh, founder of *taʿlimite* Batinism, a new form of Ismailism, sent emissaries against the sunnite Moslems.

Among these there were assassins whose most famous victims were Niẓām al-Mulk, Wazir to Sulṭān Malikshāh, and his son, Fakhr al-Mulk. It had been the custom of the learned Nizām al-Mulk to have among his court a group of famous jurists and theologians. By teaching Shāfi'ism and Ash'arism they provided a counterforce against the Shi'ism of the Fātimides in favor of the sunnite Abbasids and the Seljukides. To this end he founded many schools, led by that in Baghdad. It was precisely as director of this school that he appointed al-Ghazālī in 484/1091. In the religio-political complex of Islam at that time, this was the critical post.

LIFE OF AL-GHAZĀLĪ

The earliest biography of al-Ghazālī is by 'Abdul al-Ghāfīr al-Fārisī[3] who knew personally Muhammad son of Muhammad son of Muhammad Abū Hāmid al-Ghazālī. Al-Ghazālī was born in Tūs (450/1058) and began his studies in *fiqh* (Islamic law) there in the school of Rādkāna. Thence, he moved to Forjān under Abū'l-Qāsim al-Ismā'īlī. Finally he became an outstanding student at Nīshāpūr under, among others, al-Juwaynī, sunnite Imām al-Haramayn. His studies included law, jurisprudence, dialectics, religion and logic, reading works on hikma and *falsafah*.

After some time he experienced some distaste for the abstract sciences and turned toward the Sufi religious approach under Fāramdhī (died 477), one of the most famous shaykhs of the time. Though al-Ghazālī followed the religious practices of cult and ejaculatory prayer and overcame the obstacles, he did not achieve the religious experiences he sought, so he returned to the abstract sciences.

In epistemology he held all proofs to be equally valid, which left him bemired in casuistry: a brilliant dilettante, but without bases for certitude regarding the three great truths, namely, the existence of God, the last judgment, and prophecy. *Fiqh* does not justify these fundamental beliefs, but supposes them. Al-Ghazālī excelled in reasoning and argumentation and early began to write his own works. But this dilettantism may have been the reason why his famous teacher al-Juwaynī came to be somewhat put off by the brilliant but aggressive argumentation of his student.

Upon the deaths of Fāramdhī and of al-Juwaynī in 478, his education was complete. He was the sole major heir to the cultural tradition of his native Khorāsān, which excelled in both thought and Sufi religious experience. Soon he joined Niẓām al-Mulk at his 'Askar or military-political base. There he brought together in brilliant discussion the many visiting leading ulemas, imāms and men of letters so that his fame spread widely. At 34 he was appointed by Niẓām head of the Niẓāmiyya School in Baghdad which he led with great distinction during 484-488 (1091-1095).

At the beginning he was still the brilliant dilettante. Later, from the position of a mature wisdom and holiness, he would apologize for the arrogance with which he pursued argumentation in that earlier, less mature period, when his search was too centered upon honor and fame.

Fārisī reports that at the Niẓāmiyya he undertook important studies in three major directions. He researched the science of the roots or sources of jurisprudence (*'ilm al-usūl*); he redeveloped the school of Shāfi'ite jurisprudence; and he practiced *al-khilāf* or comparative jurisprudence. On all of these he wrote works and acquired surpassing fame and an entourage.

This attention to sciences concerned with the concrete and the practical,[4] suggests Jabre, gave him the illusion of standing on solid ground and contributing to the realization and defence of a human-divine kingdom in this life. He had joined Niẓām al-Mulk in his battle against the threat of *Ta'limism* as a new form of shī'ite bātinism which stressed the essential importance of the teaching of the Imām.

This effort received a shattering blow on 10 Ramadan 485/-1092 when Niẓām al-Mulk, Wazir or Prime Minister of the Seljoukide Sultān and patron of al-Ghazālī, was assassinated by a young Bātinite, as would be the son of Niẓām, Fakhr al-Mulk, in 500/1107 fifteen years later.

According to Abū Bakr ibn al-'Arabī it was early the next year (486/1093-1094) that al-Ghazālī underwent a definitive conversion to Sufism and turned from the sciences of things here below to the hidden, transcendent aspects of religion. The character and content of this conversion is the centerpiece of the *Munqidh*. It is no exaggeration to say that all else in the book was chosen and ordered precisely in order to explain that conversion and the new dimension of knowledge which was opened to him by the Way of the Sufis.

It is not possible to say what weight the political facts of his day, particularly the assassination of Niẓām, had on the conversion of al-Ghazālī. He himself does not refer to them in the *Munqidh*, where he restricts himself to describing the different approaches to knowledge or religion proposed by others. He describes his own thorough investigation and critique of them and by their exclusion points to the Way of the Sufis. This step was based not simply on its being the sole remaining speculative alternative, but given the distinction of theory and practice it was necessary to move beyond speculation to a higher level of experience, which provides its own positive warranty.

Some would want to hold only to his own spiritual experience and suggest that the fear which he mentions at this time was not fear of a fate similar to that of Niẓām, but fear of God, which is the beginning of wisdom.[5] This would seem to separate al-Ghazālī from the circumstances of his time in which — in view of the role of the conflict of sunnite vs shī'ite theology as the coordinating matrices of the conflicting temporal regimes of the time — he was centrally engaged.

Further, this position separates violently soul from body to focus entirely upon the disincarnate mind. But it is no derogation of the soul and its spiritual journey to place it firmly in matter or body, in time or history. That one learns true values by reflecting on the death of others or upon the circumstances which threaten one's life is as common an occurrence as taking part in a burial or even visiting a hospital. It is not surprising then that he took up once again and with renewed vigor his earlier attempt to practice Sufism. His sincerity in this is witnessed by the decade-long ascetic retreat which he would soon take up and which he would never really abandon.

In the *Munqidh* he writes at length on a long debate within himself about making a definitive break with his present life of honor and adulation by students and leaders. Did this begin from the death of Niẓām or, as would seem more probable, had it begun before, been catalyzed by the death of Niẓām, and come to a conclusive decision in 486 AH? If so was the subsequent time in Baghdad concerned only with tactics for carrying out his decision to leave that post?

At any rate, in 488/1095 he left Baghdad as part of a plan definitively to abandon his post and the country as a whole, but letting on only that he intended to make the pilgrimage to Macca. He wandered as a hermit in Damascus, Jerusalem, Hebron (and possibly Alexandria) for nearly two years. During that time he made the 489/1095-1096, pilgrimage to Macca. Ibn al-'Arabī reports seeing him in Baghdad in Jumāda 489/1095-1096, engaged in teaching, investigating the doctrines of the philosophers and writing. If he is correct about that date, later that year al-Ghazālī made a defmitive break from Baghdad. By 491, or 492/1094 at the latest, he returned to his home in Tūs where he lived a life of prayer, worship, meditation and study.

This retreat lasted some ten years. Then the son of Niẓām al-mulk, Fakhr al-Mulk, who was trying to lay down a firm line of defence against *ta'limite* Bātinism, summoned him to return once again to his earliest teaching post at Nīshāpūr.

At this point, al-Ghazālī reports, he was coming to the conclusion that, due to the pervasive corruption in society, interior prayer was not enough; to it the work of teaching must be added. The invitation added an external impetus to his interior inclinations, and he took up his teaching once again in 499/1106. This was to be of short duration, for the following year Fakhr al-Mulk too was assassinated. Soon al-Ghazālī returned to his home in Tūs. There at the side of his home he built a school for teaching *fiqh*, which always had been his main area of teaching, as well as a Sufi monastery for those in search of prayer, spiritual learning and ascetic practice. Al-Ghazālī himself undertook for the first time intensive study of the *hadīth* or the traditions regarding the prophet. He continued writing till his very last days and passed away on Monday 14 Jumāda II, 505/1111.

WORKS

The writings of al-Ghazālī, like that of many great thinkers of his day, are very vast, both in breadth and in overall length. A few notes on the types of works might convey some sense of their scope.[6]

1. *The Islamic Sciences of fiqh and Kalām: fiqh* was the cen-

ter of his teaching and some of his writing in this field remain classics to the present day. On *Kalām* his only work is *al-'Iqtiṣād fil I'ti ād* (*The Golden Mean in Belief*), which is a fine summary of its main theological questions. He seemed to place little trust in *Kalām* or apologetic theology. Indeed, his very last work was *Iljām al-'Awāmm 'an al-Khawḍ fi 'Ilm al-Kalām* (*Restricting the Masses from Engaging in the Science of Kalām*).

2. *Against Bāṭinism*: combatting Bāṭinism, especially the Taʻlimites, was a major political and cultural campaign of the time. Al-Ghazālī played a central role in the intellectual dimension of this effort by his teaching and through a number of sharply written works.

3. *Philosophy*: al-Ghazālī speaks of the need to understand thoroughly the ideas of philosophy and in *Maqāṣid al-Falāsifah* (*The Aims of the Philosophers — Intentiones Philosophorum*) produced a classic summary of Greek logic, physics and metaphysics as presented by the Islamic philosophers of his day. The work was much used in the Middle Ages, especially in the West, as a definitive handbook of philosophy. However, al-Ghazālī's intent in the work was to lay there the groundwork for the decisive attack on philosophy which he carried out in *Tahāfut al-Falāsifah* (*The Incoherence of the Philosophers; Destructio Philosophorum*). Despite Averroes's reply in *Tahāfut al-Tahāfut* some decades later, al-Ghazālī succeeded in reorienting much of Islamic thought in a mystical Sufi direction which led to a lessening of attention to Greek philosophy at least in the West.

The *Munqidh min al-Ḍalāl*, the center of concern here, is a semi-autobiographical work. Through a tour of the intellectual horizons of the day, it leads the reader to Sufism as the only sure access to truth.

The title used here is a combination of two titles: *Al-Munqidh min al-Ḍalāl wa al-Mufṣih 'an al-Aḥwāl* (*What Saves from Error and Unveils the [Mystical] States [of the Soul]*) and *Al-Munqidh min al-Ḍalāl wa al-Muwaṣṣil ilā Dhī al-'Izza wa 'al-Jalāl* (*What Saves from Error and Unites with Power and Glory*).

4. *Spiritual Guidance*: The *Ihyā' 'Ulūm al-Dīn* (*The Revitalization of the Sciences of Religion*) is his great spiritual work. Where the *Munqidh* leads one to the Sufi Way, this work enters into detail in describing what is discovered as one proceeds along this

Way — the savored experience itself, of course, remaining beyond words. The *Ihyā'* is composed of four parts, each having ten books. Part I begins with a book on knowledge which is followed by books on "The Five Pillars of Islam", i.e., the profession of belief, the canonical prayers, almsgiving, fasting and pilgrimage. Part II concerns 'ādāt, or ways of acting regarding food, marriage, etc. Part III treats *al-muhlikāt* (the things that lead to damnation). It begins with a psychological masterpiece on the mysteries of the heart and follows with books on ascetical practices for overcoming the appetites. Part IV concerns *al-munjiyāt* (the things that lead to salvation) and constitutes his spiritual masterpiece. It treats repentance, gratitude, fear, hope, poverty, love, openness to God, spiritual awareness, the review of conscience, meditation, death and the next life. All this is written with such great beauty that McCarthy cites an ancient author to the effect that "the *Ihyā'* would supply for all Islamic literature if the latter were to be lost" for it conveys "all that is best and most appealing in Islam as a religion and as a 'revelation' of God's love for man and of the heights attainable by man's love for God."[7]

ANALYSIS OF AL-*MUNQIDH MIN AL-ḌALAL*

The Work

Al-Ghazālī wrote the *Munqidh* between 499/1106 and 500/1107 in Nīshāpūr. He was fifty years old at the time and about to return to teaching. As a personal testimony it calls to mind Augustine's *Confessions*, Descartes' *Discourse on Method* and Newman's *Apologia pro vita sua*. Its complex intellectual structure and purpose make it one of the most outstanding works of world literature. Al-Ghazālī states in the introduction that he wrote the work at the request of a brother in the faith who asked him "to reveal . . . the purpose of the sciences, the evil and the depths of the schools of thought." This could be a real account and/or a literary device; in any case, most agree that it was meant for a type of reader, not for only one individual. The work is intended to explain how he first established the bases and limits of reason, and later broke beyond reason to find the Way to definitive certitude and spiritual fulfillment. By a process of exclusion his review of the competencies and limits of *kalām*, of philosophy and of the doctrine of the ta'limites led him to Sufism. There he found the Way which could take him to the prophetic light beyond which "there was no other light on the face of the earth."[8]

Proximately, he was concernd about the Bātinites who wished to propose, as an infallible Imām, the Fatimid Caliph of Cairo. Al-Ghazālī considered this prerogative to have belonged only to Muhammad himself. Like the Ash'arites facing the Mu'tazilites two centuries earlier, he was forced to rethink sunnite dogma for himself and his contemporaries, and thereby to renew the religious spirit. It was, moveover, a task which had been prophesied to be needed at the beginning of each century.

To appreciate this project it may be helpful to look first at its structure, especially as analyzed by Farid Jabre,[9] and then to consider its meaning and accomplishment from a somewhat contrasting perspective.

General Introduction (pp. 61-63)

Al-Ghazālī notes that from his early youth, before the age of 20, he had been concerned with the problem of certitude and had examined critically all the roads leading not only to religious conviction, but even to nihilism. Rather than accept the easy but blind conformism of *taqlīd*, however, he attempted to seize the deep basic reality of things, especially of human nature itself as it opened to the divine. In this regard what he sought was certain knowledge, which he described as a state of soul so bound to, and satisfied by, its object that nothing could detach it therefrom.

*The First Crisis: Sophistry and Denial of
    All Knowledge* (pp. 65-67)

In search of this perfect certitude he turned first to sense knowledge but soon recognized the illusions it generated. When he turned to reason and its first principles, however, he had difficulty distinguishing their certitude from that which he had experienced in dreams; indeed for the Sufis the whole of this life was a dream. After two months of despair with regard to knowledge he regained confidence in the directives of reason. This confidence, however, came not as a clear deduction from any methodical reasoning, but by the light that God projected into his heart.

Evaluation of Other Ways (pp. 69-89)

Long after — his education having been completed, and now at the head of the school at Baghdad — he returned once again to this issue of certitude. Now, however, it was not merely the general question of how certitude could be had in any reasoning, rather it was how one could be bound irrevocably in blessed union with God. As truth is sought by four different groups each proposing its own path, some time after 484/1091 and over a period of years at Baghdad al-Ghazālī set about studying each in depth to see which provided the true Way to God.

1. *Kalām*: (pp. 71-72) Through the Prophet God revealed the body of true beliefs upon which depends man's happiness in this life and the next. Because some deny this and attempt to disturb the faith of the believers, an apologetic approach (the *kalām*) was developed. This seeks to argue from premises which these unbelievers do admit in order to show the contradictions into which they are led by their unbelief. *Kalām* is of little service, however, for it can serve only those with a strong sense of faith. But generally these persons limit their convictions solely to the principles of faith. In time *kalām* broadened its concerns to search into the deep reality of things through the use of such philosophical categories as substance and accidents, but it could attain little sure knowledge.

2. *Falsafah*: (pp. 73-82) Thinking that philosophy had never seriously been studied by the theologicans though it had been by Avicenna, in Baghdad al-Ghazālī spent two years reading the works of the Falāsifah and a third in organizing his thoughts. He divided the Falāsifah into three categories and quickly rejected the first two: the nihilist *Dahriyyūn* or *Zanādiqa* who deny the existence of God, and the naturalist *ṭabi 'iyyūn* who believe in a powerful and wise being, but reject life after death.

In contrast, he gave extensive attention to the third category, the theist *ilāhiyyūn*, which include especially not only the Greek philosophers, Socrates, Plato and Aristotle, but the Islamic philosophers, al-Fārābī and Avicenna. Al-Ghazālī does not propose rejecting all their positions: mathematics, logic, physics, politics and much of ethics could be accepted with care and prudence. The difficulties of the philosophers come especially in the field of metaphysics and theodicy where they did not have success in furnishing the kinds of proofs demanded by their logic.

He warns against the dangers in either totally accepting or totally rejecting the philosophers, arguing strenuously for an open attitude to truth wherever it appears. Truth is not contaminated by being juxtaposed to errors, nor does it become false when included in books which contain errors on other matters. Thus, similarities between revealed truths in his works and elements in the works of some philosophers do not render the revealed matters any less true.

In sum, however, *Falsafah* will not suffice because reason is unable to know the basic truths of things, especially (but not only) with regard to the spiritual dimension of man and this mystical union with God.

3. *The Theory of Teaching* (pp. 83-89): A competing claimant to provide a sure way to God — and one most obtrusive in his day, even to the point of assassinations — was the company of those who claimed that such truth could not at all be approached by reason, but only through instruction by a teacher, particularly by the infallible Imām of the *shī'ites*. Al-Ghazālī proceeded to develop a clearer statement of their principles than could they themselves, but he did so in order to refute them. He accepted the principles of the *ta'limites* regarding the need for a doctrine and for an infallible teacher, but turned this against them by pointing out that Muḥammad was such a teacher. More basically, however, he rejected the general skepticism regarding reason implicit in their argument and their reduction of faith to blind conformism.

With regard to the contingent social order Al-Ghazālī considered error to be always possible, but not to have eternal implications. Where teaching has been received from an infallible but now dead teacher it should be followed; otherwise jurisprudential judgement (*ijtihād*) must suffice.

With regard to the fundamental truths of belief, these exist in the *Qur'ān*, the *Sunna* and the community. As shown in his book, *The Just Balance*, these truths can be argued. But, as was true even with Muḥammad's teaching, there is no guarantee that all persons will be convinced.

Al-Ghazālī argues that the position of the *ta'limites* is not consistent, for the authority of any text which would affirm the existence and infallibility of their Imām would need to be based on prophecy and certified by miracles. The appreciation and application of such certification, however, require precisely the kind of reasoning capability rejected by that position.

The Mystical Way of Sufism (pp. 91-96)

By exclusion he then turned to the way of Sufism which he notes to be both a knowledge and, even more fundamentally, a practice which constitutes a yet deeper knowledge. As practice, its goal is detachment from all else for the purpose of attachment to God. He attained information and some understanding of Sufism by reading the works of Makkī, Muḥāsibi, Junayd, Shiblī and Bisṭāmi. But he noted that the essence of Sufism was a matter not of knowledge, but of lived experience described as savoring the truth.

Hence he had to reorient himself from an outward search for objective truth to the realization of an inward state of soul; it was not a matter of knowing the definition of detachment, but of becoming detached step by step. This spiritual turn was for him a matter of great drama and pain. He had always held the three great truths: The Existence of God, Prophecy, and Resurrection on the Last Day, and had stoutly taught and defended them. But he notes with regret that he had done so with attachment to worldly honor, even to the point of treating others harshly. If, however, eternal happiness depended not on attachment but on detachment, then he had a crucial choice to make: to remain with all the attachments of his life as leader of the school in Baghdad or to break away.

The pressure of the growing awareness of this choice over a six months period beginning from Rajah 488 progressively paralysed him to a point where he could neither speak nor eat. Then, by God's help, he was able to make the break. For the rest of his days he led a life of prayer. He was a hermit for two years in Syria and Palestine; he notes especially his time in the minaret of the mosque in Damascus. Family cares recalled him once again to his home, which he left but briefly to teach at Nīshāpūr. But with his progressive practice of the Sufi Way of self-denial, prayer and meditation in Tūs the spirit of God suffused him entirely.

He recounts the stages of the Sufi Way as the purification of the heart from all that is not God and total absorption in God through annihilation of Self. Each interior step of the heart is accompanied by a corresponding step of knowledge unveiling and contemplating the truth. These take one to a proximity with God, but this is not yet the state of inherence or true mystical union. For that it is necessary to proceed by lived, even savored, experience. This has three levels: (1) knowledge by faith or belief based on the good opinion one has of one's spiritual masters or teachers; (2) indirect knowledge by verification with the help of reasoning; (3) direct knowledge by taste, which he describes as savored in order to insist upon the subjectivity of an interior appreciation of God as present beyond any objective, exterior knowledge.

All these levels are permeated by the notion of prophecy; it is the Prophet who achieves most vividly the direct experience of God which is the goal of the Sufi Way. Hence at this point in the *Munqidh* he undertakes a detailed progressive analysis of the nature of prophecy in order to be as clear as possible regarding the way which is both truth and path, both knowledge and practice.

The Nature of Prophecy: An Urgent Human Need (pp. 97-100)

Here al-Ghazālī mounts a major effort to communicate to his readers/friend the character of the lived experience to which the Sufi Way leads. He begins with a detailed sequence of the development of the various senses, followed by the ability to discern things beyond the sense level at age seven, and then the ability to grasp abstract notions, i.e. things as necessary, possible or impossible. Finally, the eye of prophecy opens which grasps a domain beyond reason. Here reason is as insensitive as is a blind person before colors, or as is reason before the world of dreams. The capacity of the human for trans-rational experience he considers to be a special gift of God.

He treats three questions regarding prophecy: its possibility, its existence and its realization in a particular person. Its possibility is illustrated by knowledge of the laws of medicine and astrology. These are known to be true, but are not subject to rational deduction. Moreover, some dreams testify to the fact of a realm of knowledge beyond reason. Prophetic knowledge exists in the experience which can be developed by following the Way of Sufism.

Like knowledge of whether someone is authentically a doctor or jurist, recognition of the existence of prophecy in a particular person requires first some sense of the nature of prophecy. This can be had by meeting such persons and considering their teaching and actions. However, the life of the prophet is its own best witness, more than external phenomena such as changing a stick into a serpent.[10] Thus it is by being with Sufis that one comes to know that the higher experience has been attained by some and thus that it does exist and can be attained by their Way.

Practical Problems and the Return to Teaching (pp. 101-112)

The remainder of the work focuses on the practical problems or difficulties in bringing the Way into more general practice. Humans are both body and spirit or heart. The latter is the proper place of knowledge of God, but like the body it too can die if it lacks knowledge of God or falls ill through disobedience to Him. What is more, just as the body is healed by medical properties which the reason cannot understand, so the heart can be healed by practices of cult which only the higher experience of the prophet can appreciate.

Al-Ghazālī explained the nature of prophecy by leading the reader step by step toward experiences that transcend both the senses and reason. But in order to be attracted toward such a goal one needs to experience it in others. Here, the difficulty is precisely the bad examples of those supposedly learned persons who should be practicing it, or the defects of others who do attempt to practice the Way. The result is general tepidity.

Al-Ghazālī responded both in theory and in practice. Regarding theory or truth, to those whose tepidity is due to:

- *ta'limism*, as a virus aggressively promoted in his day and proposing passive dependence on an infallible Imām, al-Ghazālī directs that they read his work: *The Just Balance*.

- the teaching of the *falāsifah*, who aggressively extend the realm of reason and reduce all else in the *Qur'ān* to mere allegory, al-Ghazālī directs that they review his teaching on prophecy as transcending the capacities of reason.

- the arguments of the libertines, al-Ghazālī directs that they read his work, *The Alchemy of Happiness*.

- the claim that prophecy is only for the common people, but not for those who can understand its contents and develop an empirical ethics (*hikma*) based on God, al-Ghazālī teaches that in fact they reject prophecy because they reduce what is distinctive about it, namely, its transcendence of reason, to the level of a sage usage of reason.

Moreover, al-Ghazālī is conscious that holiness as an inner reality can be betrayed above all from within, that those who should exemplify the experiences achieved from the Way may be impeded in so doing by various temptations, and therefore generate scandal rather than being beacons for others. Al-Ghazālī attempts to protect against this by asserting: (1) that all have knowledge of the difference between good and evil and should not be misled by anyone who falls before temptations, which, after all, everyone experiences, and (2) that knowledge of the Way is itself a corrective for it directs one to repent and move on, not to remain in sin.

But al-Ghazālī had a practical response to make as well. Seeing that tepidity seemed to be spreading he became convinced that a strenuous effort at education was needed. He made a last effort in that direction by accepting the invitation of the son of Niẓām to take charge of the school at Nīshāpūr. When this approach was cut short by the assassination of his patron, he moved his effort to his home in Tūs, where he built a school and monastery to teach and promote the practice of Sufism.

MEANING OF THE *MUNQIDH*

The above analysis of the text attempted to follow closely its structure. The text, however, is not simply autobiographical, but a somewhat stylized ordering of the elements of his life and hence of his Sufi experience. In this his goal, he says, is to respond to the question of the purpose of the related sacred sciences and the evil and depth of the relevant schools of thought. Hence, in order further to unfold the import of the *Munqidh* it may help to add here some reflections upon the different philosophical issues involved.

Epistemology

The issue of knowledge[11] and its competencies is basic here, for his purpose is to show not only what reason can do in order progressively to lead toward the Way, but even more what reason cannot do in order, through contrast, to make manifest what is distinctive and indispensable in the mystical Way of the Sufis. Moreover, beyond the issue of the way to personal perfection, al-Ghazālī's understanding of knowledge played a significant role in his work *The Incoherence of the Philosophers (Tahāfut al-Falāsifah)*, which helped to orient Islamic scholarship into more mystical channels.

In terms of present-day concerns, this may relate, on the one hand, to the troubled history of the relation of Islam to the processes of modernization derived from the scientific elaboration of reason. On the other hand, it may relate also to the mystical direction of Islamic thought and its potential for contributing to the present renewal of the search for spiritual meaning in response to the loss of meaning in our increasingly rationalized society.[12]

To see how this can be so one should note with Farid Jabre that while the work was written toward the end of al-Ghazālī's life its literary point of view is rather that of the period of his leadership of the school at Baghdad. Particularly, it reflects the point at which he comes seriously to investigate the adequacy of the sciences and schools of thought. In this light the work — and his life — clearly divide into two parts: the first is preliminary and is devoted to the basis for scientific reasoning, the second main section is devoted to questioning these bases with a view to showing the need, the nature and the goal of the Way of the Sufis.

Each phase is marked by a personal crisis, the first of which foreshadows the second. McCarthy downplays the first as the relatively universal step of the late adolescent forced to take up responsibility for his or her own capacity of knowledge.[13] In contrast, Jabre,[14] as it were, places a magnifying glass on this first crisis in order to uncover much more precisely the nature of the epistemology which al-Ghazālī developed for human reason. This would remain with him throughout his life and would be the point of reference against which he would delineate the further step to the mystical and the prophetic.

Moreover, because al-Ghazālī later notes that he never doubted the great truths of the faith, Jabre would distinguish this first crisis from Descartes's universal doubt and limit it to the motives of credibility of faith before the judgment of reason. But if Descartes could stress the importance of keeping one's fundamental beliefs even while applying the technique of his methodic doubt,[15] the young al-Ghazālī could claim to have done no less in his own general state of initial confusion.

Jabre would focus al-Ghazālī's early crisis on the rational means or motives which justify belief and consider that this defines all that follow. In contrast, al-Ghazālī himself seems to describe it as a preliminary crisis regarding the validity of reason. This is but a shadow of the general epistemological question which he develops later in the main body of the text. There he treats of the ability of reason to achieve the real nature or, by spatial analogy, the deep reality (*haqīq*a or pulp) of things as opposed to merely their surface appearance.

To this spatial analogy of levels on the part of the object, there corresponds in al-Ghazālī's thought a parallel set of levels on the part of the self. The deepest level is the transrational goal of the Sufis, but this can be illumined through contrast to the more surface or preliminary levels, which are those of sense and reason that al-Ghazālī lists in his section on prophecy. Let us attempt a more precise delineation of his notion of reason. This could provide insight not only into his perception of the goal of the mystical Way, but also into the limitation of the sciences. The *Tahāfut* explains his break from the earlier Islamic work on Greek philosophy and hence the broader turn of Islamic scholarship toward a mystical path.

In Aristotle's logic, which ruled his development of the structure of the sciences, all begins from first principles such as that of non-contradiction first sketched by Parmenides. These have absolute and universal value from the beginning of the work of reason. In this light, by a process of induction from the particular to the universal, the natures of things are abstracted. With these the deductive syllogisms are constructed in the various sciences, each with their distinctive universal principles.

Jabre suggests that al-Ghazālī took only the form of such syllogistic reasoning (via the Arabic *qiyās*), and into this form poured a quite different content. Reasoning was not simply the results of induction from concrete sense experience, even in the cases of the positive sciences; for al-Ghazālī the intellect does see, but its objects are not simply human constructs. Absolute judgments regarding the necessary, the possible and the impossible are always present, but with regard to other judgments the human intellect is only a capacity. Hence, it needs to be enlightened by the *hikma*, of which the greatest is the word of God, especially the *Qur'ān* by which vision is accomplished.

What then of "the first principles"? For al-Ghazālī these are grasped directly in and of themselves; they have an unchangeable character which is imposed with necessity upon the mind. Their purpose is to prepare the mind by providing an anticipated experience of necessity, which truly belongs only to God and the truth of the Prophet. Despite even this, however, they could yet be considered a mirage or illusion, for their definitive truth is possessed only when they are envisaged in terms of — that is, in and by — Islam.

To understand this seeming affirmation and yet negation of the competency of reason it is necessary to recall that epistemology is essentially dependent upon metaphysics for an understanding of the nature and origin of knowledge, since that too is a reality and subject to the laws of being. McCarthy points out that in his metaphysics al-Ghazālī was always a convinced occasionalist. God in creating nature and humankind remained the one truly Real Being and hence the source of all action. Humans may act, but the reality or being of the effect was the result not of human activity, but of God. For knowledge this means that man may think, but that the reality of knowledge and truth is the effect not of humans, but of God.

An intermediate position was held by the Christian Platonists of the School of St. Augustine for whom a special light or illumination was needed in order to explain the universality and necessity of the human knowledge which man drew from particular and changing reality. In response to this position, it was the contribution of Thomas Aquinas to appreciate that the power of God implied that His creatures be self-sufficient. This meant that in their own (created) right they possessed all the competencies needed in order to realize all the actions which were in accord with their nature.[16] This extended the power of God proportionately and by participation to all His work.

(This was an important corrective by Thomas to one of the main defects which al-Ghazālī found in Ibn Rushd [Averroes]. Al-Ghazālī was concerned that too close a following of Aristotle led Averroes to attenuate the reality of the individual's spiritual soul and hence to an inadequate affirmation of the Resurrection on the Last Day. This al-Ghazālī classified as heretical.)[17]

For al-Ghazālī the conviction that the realization of truth was the effect of God, not of man, meant that the first truths could be looked upon in two ways. If seen in relation to the truth about God and constituting part of knowledge about God, they received therefrom truly definitive power.

The first principles could, however, be looked upon in another way, namely, as principles for any reasoning to God, or indeed for any reasoning whatsoever. Such knowledge is not certain. This is expressed by the phrase "the equivalence of proofs" (*takāfu' al-adilla*) indicating that "falsehood on the part of a proof does not entail the falsity of the object it proves." It can apply either to the necessary principles and to all properly speculative knowledge or only to the latter, all of which it blankets with doubt.

Up to 28 years of age, during the period when al-Ghazālī was introduced to philosophy, *kalām*, *fiqh* and all the sciences, his mind was molded according to this pattern by his teacher, Juwaynī, who was among the initiators of this view, which Ibn Khaldūn considers the distinguishing doctrine between "the ancients" and "the moderns". It is not surprising then that al-Ghazālī would be the one to write the *Tahāfut al-Falāsifah* (*Incoherence of the Philosophers*) criticizing elements of the Islamic strain of Greek philosophy. Averroes's belated effort to answer in his *Tahāfut al tahāfut* (*Incoherence of the Incoherence*) was destined beforehand to be ineffective, for no reasoned reply could be effective when reason was no longer held to provide knowledge that was certain.

The Metaphysics of Mysticism

Al-Ghazālī's epistemology did not change in the second period of his life, beginning from the age of 34 when he was placed in charge of the Niẓāmiyya School in Baghdad. Writing as he does from this epistemological perspective, Farid Jabre tends to downplay the philosophical significance of this second period.[18] He sees it as but a repetition of the first period, though now in psychological and phenomenal terms describing al-Ghazālī's lived experience of the limitation of reason. To McCarthy, however, it is just the opposite; having reduced al-Ghazālī's first crisis to being simply the universal experience of passing from adolescence, McCarthy places all the meaning in the second phase of his life,[19] which all agree to be the main focus of the *Munqidh*.

It is suggested here that the truth lies between these two positions.[20] That is, the main lines of his epistemology can indeed be traced in the earlier period, as Jabre has effectively done. He is correct in observing that during that earlier period al-Ghazālī did not advance beyond the realm of reason and that it lacked definitive certainty. But if that be so certainly something of the greatest moment takes place when in the second period he does actively apply himself to the Way that leads beyond reason. He identifies its veracity, and then applies himself in a ten-year retreat to the assiduous practice of the Way from which results his *Iḥyā' 'Ulūm al-Dīn* (*The Revitalization of the Sciences of Religion*), the landmark of Islamic spirituality. This is hardly a mere "répétition de la première . . . sous un autre form,"[21] as claims Jabre. That failure to appreciate the distinctive reality of the achievement of the second phase of al-Ghazālī's life would seem to result from seeing it only in psychological terms as the flow of phenomena of a human order. It must be appreciated rather in the metaphysical terms, e.g., of a Heidegger, as the unveiling of Being Itself through the intentional life of *dasein*, or in the properly mystical terms which McCarthy approaches with great respect, even awe, as before a sanctuary of the divine. This enables McCarthy to grasp the tremendous fascination of the religious event lived by al-Ghazālī and described in the main body of his text.[22]

If the *Munqidh* has a consistent message it is that at its highest reason remains insufficient, and that even in its efforts to defend religion in the *Kalām* it is weak and largely ineffectual.

One cannot come to the reality of the divine in the depth of the human heart by mere belief according to dogmatic formulae, for these remain surface, brittle and subject to dissolution. The approach to the divine is rather by ascetic and ritual practices which progressively remove the chains that bind the heart so as to allow it to open before the corresponding unveiling of the divine. It is in this that one comes to certain knowledge (*yaqīn*), rising above religious conformism (*taqlīd*) through actively savoring the experience of God. Here reason, as prepared by the practices of cult and informed by meditation upon the prophetic teaching, has only to reflect upon itself as a concrete reality.

In contrast to the objective and relatively exterior stance of pure speculative reason which can lead only to *Ijtihād*, al-Ghazālī insists that in the mystical Way of the Sufi's the divine is seized immediately and savored. He stresses thus the interiority and lived subjectivity of this process. This emphasis accords with his description of certainty as a state of soul so bound to, and satisfied by, its object that nothing could detach it therefrom. Even more, it is mystical union with God and definitive fulfillment, of which such certainty is but a sign.

Here, al-Ghazālī is cautious. He explicitly rejects that this nearness to God constitutes an in-dwelling, total union or eastern type of fusion, for none of these would protect the unicity of God. The mystical presence is beyond what can be described in terms of the relation of two within the same set, for there is no parity whatsoever between God and man. Hence nobody can attempt to express these states without failing miserably. "Whatever has happened, I shall not speak of it. . . . Do not question me about it" (ch. III).

Yet neither is a via negative by itself sufficient to reflect the inexpressible intimacy which the mystic experiences with the divine. This is the goal of the Way, the very title of this work: *Deliverance from Error and Mystical Union with the Almighty*; it is the throbbing, vital center which enlivens, inspires and transforms all of being and life.

In this light it is possible to appreciate more deeply the meaning of the *Munqidh*. It is not only a gripping account of a psychological drama with deep sonorities lived by al-Ghazālī in Baghdad. His discovery, upon their review, that all other ways were wanting — philosophy, *kalām* and especially *ta'līm* — and his being led thereby to the Sufi Way of self-abnegation and mystical union with God was not only the progression of the life of one person. Beyond this it is a description of the Way of continued emergence of the divine in time through prophecy and of the opening of hearts thereto through the mystical path. It is truly an account of God with us, which transforms human life and history.

One who appreciated the implications of this less thoroughly and less deeply than al-Ghazālī would have worked out some pragmatic compromise allowing him to stay in Baghdad — after all, as a spiritually sensitive director he would be better for the school than he had been when he acted too much on the basis of human reason and for the too human motives of fame and honor. It is testimony to his sincerity and charity that he could not act on the basis of any such compromise. In turn, this suggests responses to problems raised from a number of directions.

Al-Ghazālī himself was conscious that some would suggest that he was being led by his ego to attempt to become the reformer of his century, according to the prophecy that each century would begin with a major reformer.[23] But if ever human reason could conceive such a hope it would certainly be based upon his position as director of the great Niẓāmiyya school in Baghdad, not as a hermit enclosed in the minaret of the mosque at Damascus or in his hometown of Ṭūs.

Others would cite his phrase that all his prior life had been led by the search for fame, that his teaching "had not been directed towards God the Almighty alone . . . (but to) seek glory and renown."[24] Based on this they would question the sincerity of his conversion and hence of this account.[25] But the remark would be meaningless except in the context of a conversion from such motivation.

Similarly, there are those who would question the sincerity of Descartes's references to God and in effect eviscerate Books III-V of his *Meditations* in order to protect the forced reductionism of their materialist reading of Books II and VI. Also, there are critics who, in order to protect their own overly literal and out-of-context reading of a very few lines, reject the seriousness of al-Ghazālī's account of his conversion and by implication the authenticity of the whole teaching of his massive *Ihyā' 'Ulūm ad-Dīn*. But they must be guided by something other than al-Ghazālī's text or his life.

Still others[26] would see his departure from Baghdad not in the spiritual terms in which he depicts it, but rather as fear generated by the assassination of his sponsor, Niẓām al-Mulk. Certainly, the Niẓāmiyya school at Baghdad was the key intellectual battlefield and al-Ghazālī was its key figure. He does not hide the element of fear, which was quite natural in the circumstances. But al-Ghazālī places it within the context of the much broader and deeper sweep of the challenge of conversion in his life. Undoubtedly, the assassination of the patron of his School was too great and threatening a happening to be ignored, but this account, written when he was an advanced Sufi, naturally describes all in terms of his awareness of the Providence of God, rather than as simply the machinations of mere humans. The description of his life is in terms of his search for the Way and of what can be communicated of this that has meaning for a broad class of readers interested in the Way to truth. In these terms the assassinations and other turmoils of his particular time are of marginal importance.

It might be noted further that even late in his ten year period of retreat, when he was considering how to respond to the tepidity abroad in Islam, he considered it important to have an authoritative patron. This could be taken as an issue of protection, but it seems more probable that it was considered important as an element in the plan of Nizām to develop an alliance of faith and political power which could protect against Batinism and promote the Sunnī Islamic faith. The assassination of Nizām al-Mulk meant, of course, the sudden collapse of this worldly hope. The *Munqidh* then may not be adequate history. But the work has survived because it focused not upon surface events that happen only once, but upon what is essential in the human pilgrimage and gives it ultimate meaning.

One would hope then that he would have written much more extensively here about his lived experience of the Way during his retreat following his departure from Baghdad. But, of course, he has done this brilliantly and in the greatest detail in the 40 books of the *Ihyā'*; it is there that one must turn for the enduring harvest of his leap of faith.

THE IMPACT OF THE *MUNQIDH*: PAST AND PRESENT

For Islam the impact of the *Munqidh* was decisive, especially if one includes the pattern of work it reflects. This includes al-Ghazālī's decisive critique of philosophy in the *Tahāfut*, his description of the discovery of the mystical way though a critique of the sciences, including *kalām*, in the *Munqidh* itself, and the massively imposing *Ihyā'* with its detailed exposition of the spiritual wisdom gained from his long Sufi retreat. It is not without reason that al-

Ghazālī has been described as the greatest Muslim after Muḥammad himself.

As the classical sciences of *kalām* and *fiqh* had come to appear respectively as too apologetic and too external, there was urgent need to renew access to the religious wellsprings of Islam. The obvious candidate for such an expedition was reason. This had been developed to a high state by the Greeks, whose major works had been translated into Arabic. It had been richly developed by such ingenious Islamic thinkers as al-Fārābī, Ibn Sīnā (Avicenna) and Ibn Rushd (Averroes). But was reason enough — particularly as developed in terms of a culture of the ancient Greek gods, rather than of the revelation of the One God? Three responses were possible.

The first, by Ibn Sīnā and Ibn Rushd, each in his own distinct way, was that reason could be of great assistance in this effort to discover the religious meaning of life and to order all life in that light. Indeed, their great works illustrate this point so well that no external certification of their significance need be added to that which shines from within.

There is, however, a fatal weakness in human reason. As human it is limited and can never be adequate to the divine which transcends it. Yet, as reason it looks for universal principles and laws which order all and render all intelligible to a limited mind. This tension shows up most in the Platonic and neo-Platonic line of Greek reasoning upon which, especially, the Islamic philosophers drew. The result was a tendency to tailor such realities as the "assemblage" or "resurrection" of the body on the last day and the personal spiritual principle to categories which were not really adequate to the task. Al-Ghazālī drew up a list of twenty such points, three of which he cites in the *Munqidh*. Al-Ghazālī's judgment in the *Tahāfut* that this avenue was simply too dangerous to the integrity of revelation and should effectively be abandoned was broadly accepted, despite the later protestations of Averroes.

The second response was that of al-Ghazālī himself. In three years of work on the philosophers he quite mastered their thought and indeed wrote one of its major summaries for his time, the *Maqāsid al-Falāsifah*. In the end he felt, nonetheless, that he needed to abandon that avenue as well as *Kalām* and, of course, the position of the *ta'līmites*, and by exclusion he could see clearly that he must devote himself to the mystical Way of the Sufis. This led precisely beyond objective reason to an interior path of abnegation until his heart could open to God in a manner so intimate and life giving that it could actively be savored but not articulated.

The impact upon Islam of this step, so effectively presented in the *Munqidh,* was of the highest order. Matching the turn away from Greek philosophy, there came a new appreciation of the spiritual and mystical dimension of Islam. However, while al-Ghazālī's work leaves no question about the need to go beyond the sciences in faith, it is not iconoclastic. That is, its objective is not to destroy these sciences or to dissuade people from their study. He is at pains to plead against this and to stress the need to look for truth everywhere, to accept it wherever it is found, and to recognize that it can be found even in the presence of error. Hence, upon discovering for himself the Sufi Way he remained ever the teacher of *fiqh,* and indeed returned to that work formally at the end of his life.

In assessing the impact of al-Ghazālī's life, then, scholars speak of it not as an attack on the sacred sciences, but as aiding to overcome their arid scholasticism, as narrowing the gulf between them and the wellsprings of the spirit, and even as discovering ways to infuse new life into the old sciences.

To this should be added then a corrective of the commonplace that scholarship ended with, and even by, al-Ghazālī Though this may be true largely of the Islamic study of Greek philosophy especially in the West, scholarship in Islam took on a new mode. Spiritually it became more deep and rich and corresponded more to the intensive life of faith of the people. Or perhaps this should be put the other way round, namely, that al-Ghazālī's strong religious mark on the subsequent cultural history of Islam reflects, second only to Muhammad himself, the spiritual pilgrimage made by al-Ghazālī and described in his *Munqidh.*

If so, this certainly is due in part to the fact that al-Ghazālī recognized, explored and effectively presented a dimension of Islam not previously given so great relief. Some, writing from the individualistic Anglo-Saxon perspective, refer to this as an individualization of the Islamic faith, but the closed, self-centered character of individualism hardly does justice to the Sufi Way through the self to the Infinite source and goal of all. By abnegation one truly dies to self in order to be opened to the transcendent. Hence it would be more true to speak not of an individualization, but of a personalization of the life of faith. This would no longer be the affair only of great leaders — caliphs or sultāns — but of the millions of persons who practice this religion. And if these cultic practices are carried out in unison by large bodies of persons they are seen by al-Ghazālī as making the heart flexible and nimble for the Way which each can follow toward the mystical union with God stated in the title of this work. In other words, all was given new life by al-Ghazālī's work which described the Way to the divine Source and Goal of life itself. In turn, this marks the character of each of the faithful and hence of the community of believers, Islam, as a whole.

There is, however, a possible third response to the relation of reason to this path of faith. We have seen the first response, that of Ibn Sīnā and Ibn Rushd, which gave primacy to reason in an attempt to reconcile it with faith. We saw also the second response, that of al-Ghazālī, which did not move against reason, but was concerned above all with how this needed to be transcended in the Way to God.

The third response comes not from Islam, but from Christianity which held in high honor the works of the Arabic philosophers. In the Christian medieval context there were both those who greatly admired this philosophy and others who, with al-Ghazālī, pointed to its defects with regard to the spiritual dimension of the person, resurrection, etc. It was the proper contribution of Thomas Aquinas a century later to work out a resolution of these problems. He did so neither by simply repeating Aristotle nor by abandoning his metaphysics, but by appreciating the deepened sense of being unveiled by a cultural context marked by faith. His creative work to heal the discrepancies between Greek philosophy and a faith-filled vision of life and meaning could be considered quite properly a continuation of the work of the Islamic philosophers.

On the one hand, the thrust of medieval Christian philosophers such as Aquinas was not to oppose al-Ghazālī, as had Ibn Rushd in his *Tahāfut al Tahāfut*. Though they lacked most of al-Ghazālī's work they shared his concern for the literal integrity of the faith. Like al-Ghazālī, they acknowledged the inadequacy of Greek thought for the vision of man in this world and the next which had emerged under the light of faith. They went about the creative and properly philosophical work of resolving these conflicts by developing philosophy itself. In this sense they moved philosophy forward in an era of faith, Islamic and Christian.

On the other hand, with the philosophers, Thomas acknowledged the need to reconcile reason and faith, rather than simply to surpass reason. For though faith was more than reason, it did not contradict reason, but was aided by it. Thus, the work of Thomas included very detailed commentaries on the works of Aristotle, which reflect significantly those of Averroes. Aquinas's *Disputed Questions* and *Summa Theologiae* constitute also a detailed philosophy of the human person and an ethics.

While Thomas thus provided the context in which a spiritual theology could be constructed, it is notable that R. Garrigou Lagrange, an eminent Thomist, in actually carrying out such a construction drew notably on the mystic experience of Theresa of Avila and John of the Cross.[27] This may suggest that this third alternative of Thomas Aquinas did not succeed in adequately integrating the first approach by objective reason with the second by mystical interiority, and that al-Ghazālī's work has a further major role to play in any such integration.

Nevertheless, this third response by Thomas Aquinas, by resolving the problems which al-Ghazalī saw in the response of Ibn Sīnā and Ibn Rushd, made it possible to continue to mine the vein of Islamic-Greek philosophy with its primacy on reason. This opened the way for developments which before long would evolve into the development of the sciences and their accompanying technology that have characterized the modern age. Indeed, to the degree that the modern developments of scientific thought are especially Platonic in character they correspond more to the Platonic character of Islamic philosophy than to the ultimately Aristotelian character of Thomas's own thought.

Commonly it is noted, however, that in modern times attention to reason has degenerated into rationalism, accompanied by a desiccating lack of adequate attention to the life of the spirit. Indeed, the triumphs of rationalism in the 20th century have been characterized by an oppressive totalitarianism and a deadening consumerism. These deficiencies of rationalism call for al-Ghazālī's clear proclamation of the distinctive character of the spirit, and of the Way which leads thereto. Healing our times must begin with the Spirit and the Way, for only in their higher light can we face the unfinished task of working out the relation of reason to the fullness of the human spirit.

This suggests then that the goal of al-Ghazālī for our times would be that reason be inspired by, and directed to, life in the Spirit. This, in turn, would enable the progress of reason truly to serve men and women, not only as images, but indeed as intimates of God. This is the central message of al-Ghazālī's *Munqidh*, if not for his day, then certainly for ours.[28]

NOTES

1. Richard Joseph McCarthy, *Freedom and Fulfillment* (Boston: Twayne, 1980), pp. xii-xiii.

2. (Chicago: The University of Chicago Press, 1974), 3 vols, especially the Introduction and General Prologue in Vol. I, pp. 30-99.

3. McCarthy, pp. xiv-xx.

4. Farid Jabre in al-Ghazālī, *Al-Munqidh min Aḍḍalāl* (*Erreur et Délivrance*) trans., intro., notes par Farid Jabre (Beyrouth: Commision Internationale pour la Traduction des Chefs-d'Oeuvre, 1959), pp. 21-22.

5. McCarthy, pp. xxxv xlii.

6. *Ibid.*, pp. xxi-xxiv; Jabre, p. 53.

7. *Ibid.*, pp. xxiii.

8. *Munqidh*, chapter 4.

9. Jabre, pp. 27-41.

10. Gerald Stanley, "Contemplation as Fulfillment of the Human Person", in George F McLean, ed., *Personalist Ethics and Human Subjectivity*, Vol. II of *Ethics at the Crossroads* (Washington, D.C.: The Council for Research in Values and Philosophy, 1995), appendix, pp. 365.

11. Jabre, pp. 41-51.

12. V. Havel, "Address in Philadelphia", July 4, 1994 in *The Washington Post*, July 6, A 19.

13. McCarthy, pp. 121-122, nn. 43-44.

14. Farid Jabre, pp. 41-47.

15. R. Descartes, *Discourse on Method*, III.

16. G.F. McLean, "Philosophic Continuity and Thomism" in *Teaching Thomism Today* (Washington: Catholic University, 1963), pp. 23-28.

17. *Munqidh,* chapter 2, part 2.

18. Jabre, p. 48.

19. McCarthy, p 121, n. 43.

20. Hodgson, vol. II, p. 186, n. 18, points insightfully in this direction noting that the philosophy/theology of Paul Tillich may be the best modern correspondent to the thought of al-Ghazālī on how "reason leads to the need for ultimate faith, but awaits revelation to carry it further. . . . (This) is not a matter of supplementing reason on its own level, but of complementing it in total experience." See also G.F. McLean, *Ways to God* (Washington: The Council for Research in Values and Philosophy, 1999), ch. X.

21. Jabre, p. 48.

22. McCarthy, pp. lvi-lx.

23. McCarthy, pp. xxvi-xxix.

24. *Munqidh,* chap. 2, part 3.

25. 'Abdul al-Da 'im al-Baqarī, *I'tirāfāt al-Ghazālī, aw kayfa 'avrakla al-Ghazālī nafsahu* (The Confessions of al-Ghazālī) (Cairo: 1943). See McCarthy, pp. xxvi-xxix.

26. F. Jabre, *al-Munqidh,* pp. 22-23. See McCarthy's response, pp. xxxv-xlii.

27. R. Garrigou Lagrange, *Christian Perfection and Contemplation according to St. Thomas Aquinas and St. John of the Cross,* trans. M.T. Doyle (London: Herder, 1937); *The Three Ages of the Interior Life, Prelude to Eternal Life,* trans. M.T. Doyle (London: Herder: 1947).

28. G.F. McLean, *Faith, Reason and Philosophy;* appendix: *The Encyclical Letter of Pope John Paul II,* Fides et Ratio (Washington, D.C.: The Council for Research in Values and Philosophy, 2000).

Al-Ghazālī

DELIVERANCE
FROM ERROR
AND
MYSTICAL UNION
WITH
THE ALMIGHTY

A Translation of
al-Munqidh min al-Ḍalāl
by Muḥammad Abūlaylah

INTRODUCTION

In the name of God, Merciful Benefactor, Praise be to God —
with such praise every message and prayer should begin — and
blessed be Muḥammad, His chosen prophet and messenger: Blessings be upon his kin and companions who have guided people away
from error.[1]

My brother in faith,[2] you have asked me to reveal to you the
purpose and secrets[3] of the sciences, and the dangerous and complex
depths of the schools of thought. You would like me to tell you
what I have undergone in order to distinguish the truth[4] from error
in the different sects, despite the differences in their paths and methods.

You wish to know the daring it took to rise above the plain of
conformism (*Taqlīd*)[5] to the heights of observation and independent
investigation.[6] First, what profit I drew at the beginning from
Kalām[7] (or theology). Secondly, how I then turned away from those
who defended *Ta'līm*[8] (teaching) because they were impeded in
reaching the truth by their subjection to the Imām.[9] Thirdly, how
much I mistrusted the methods of philosophers,[10] and finally how I
came to appreciate the way of Sufism.[11]

You would like to see the "pulp of the truth" as it appeared to
me after I had doubled my efforts to analyze what different people
said, and you would like to know what caused me to abandon my
teaching in Baghdad despite the great number of my pupils there,
and what made me take it up again, a long time later, in Nīshāpūr.[12]
I promptly fulfilled your wishes, which I recognize as sincere, and,
counting on God to grant aid, confidence, success and protection I
now plunge into my subject.

You should know — may God set you on the right path, and
lead you gently towards the truth — that people have different reli-
gions and beliefs, that there are different theological systems among
religious leaders, and that the community of Islam has different
sects and paths. All of this constitutes a deep sea in which most
have foundered and only a few have survived. Yet each group believes it has found salvation, "each party rejoices at what it possesses."[13] This was accomplished by what the Master of prophets —
peace be upon him — foretold sincerely and truthfully when he
said: "My nation will divide into seventy-three sects, and only one

of them will be saved."[14] What he foretold has indeed almost come true.

As for myself, since my early youth when I reached puberty, and before twenty, up to the present time when I am over fifty, I have not ceased to delve into the depths of the deep ocean (of the various beliefs of humankind), to plunge into its depths boldly, not as a cautious coward; to bury myself in obscure questions, eagerly seizing upon difficulties and leaping bravely into difficult and obscure issues; and to scrutinize the beliefs of each sect, examining from the doctrinal point of view the hidden aspects of every religious group.

I do this in order to distinguish those who promote truth from those who advocate falsehood, and the faithful follower of the *Sunna* (tradition) from the innovator.[15] I do not leave an "interiorist" (Bātinī)[16] without attempting to discover his doctrine, or a "literalist" (Zāhirī) without seeking to know the essentials of his belief. I want to know the real thought of the "philosopher" (Faylasuf);[17] I try to understand the purpose of the "theologian's" (Mutakallim)[18] discussion and argumentation. I wish to penetrate the secrets of the "mystic" (Sufi); I observe the devotee and what he gains from his severe devotion, as well as the nihilist materialist (Zindīq)[19] in order to discover the reasons for his bold attitude.

From my youngest years in the prime of life, my thirst to seize the profound reality of things was a natural instinct or tendency which God placed in me not by my choice or conscious decision. As I approached adolescence, while still young, the traditional bonds had already loosened and my inherited tendencies[20] had broken down. I perceived that Christian children grew up as Christians, young Jews grew up in Judaism, and young Muslims in Islam. I had heard the tradition (*hadīth*)[21] that the Prophet — peace be upon him — said: "Everyone is born with a sound nature (*fitra*),[22] it is one's parents who make one into a Jew, a Christian or a Magian."[23]

An interior force drove me to research the reality of original human nature, and that of the beliefs which derive from conformism to the authority of parents and teachers. I tried to discern among the elements which are taught by rote and accepted without question, nor yet give rise to so much controversy between the seekers of truth and the advocates of falsehood.[24]

Then I said to myself, "My aim is to perceive the deep reality of things; I wish to seize the essence of knowledge. Certain knowledge is that in which the thing known reveals itself without leaving any room for doubt or any possibility of error or illusion, nor can the heart allow such a possibility.[25] One must be protected from error, and should be so bound to certainty that any attempt, for example, to transform a stone into gold or a stick into a serpent would not raise doubts or engender contrary probabilities. I know very well that ten is more than three. If anyone tries to dissuade me by saying, 'No, three is more than ten,' and wants to prove it by changing in front of me this stick into a serpent, even if I saw him changing it, still this fact would engender no doubt about my knowledge. Certainly, I would be astonished at such a power, but I would not doubt my knowledge.

Thus, I came to know that whatever is known without this kind of certainty is doubtful knowledge, not reliable and safe; that all knowledge subject to error is not sure and certain.

CHAPTER I

THE WAYS OF SOPHISTRY
AND THE DENIAL OF
ALL KNOWLEDGE[26]

However, when I examined what I know, I found myself lacking this kind of certain knowledge, except as concerned things I could confirm with my senses[27] or those which are necessary (self-evident) for reason.[28]

So I said, "Now that despair has overcome me, there is no point in studying any problems except on the basis of what is self-evident, namely, the affirmations of the senses and the necessary truths of reason." I had to look clearly at the nature of my trust in what I could confirm with my senses, and my confidence in being safe from error by following the requirements of reason. Are these feelings similar to my previous trust in the opinions of authority[29] and the feeling of most people regarding speculative knowledge?[30] Or is it a question of a certainty without illusion or surprise?

I proceeded therefore most earnestly to consider the evidence of my senses and the requirements of reason to see if I could make myself doubt these. This led me to lose faith in the evidence of my senses. This doubt, which became completely pervasive, can be expressed as follows:

How can one trust the evidence of one's senses? Sight is the most powerful of our senses, and we could stare at a shadow and judge that it is fixed and not moving at all. Yet, at the end of an hour's watching, we find that the shadow has moved, not all at once, but gradually or little by little: it has been moving all the time, and never was in a state of rest. The eye looks at a star and sees it reduced to the size of a coin (dinar), whereas geometrical computations show it to be larger than the earth. This and similar cases exemplify how the evidence of one's senses leads one to a judgment which reason shows irrefutably to be totally erroneous.

Thus, I told myself that there is no security even in the evidence of one's senses. Perhaps such surety can be found only in intellectual truths which play the role of first principles of thought, such as: ten is greater than three; the same thing cannot simultaneously be affirmed and denied; nothing here below can be both created and eternal, existent and non-existent, necessary and impossible.[31]

But the evidence of my senses replied, are you sure that when you trust the requirements of reason it is not the same sort of trust that you had in the evidence of your senses? You trusted us, then reason accused us of being in error; without that word of reason, you would trust us still. Perhaps there is something beyond reason which would show that reason in turn is in error, just as reason showed the error of the evidence of the senses. The fact that this further intelligence is not manifest does not prove that it is impossible.

I remained for some little time speechless. Then the difficulty appeared to resemble the problem of sleep. I told myself that when one is asleep one believes all sorts of things and finds oneself in all sorts of situations; one believes in them absolutely, without the slightest doubt. When one wakes up, one realizes the inconsistency and inanity of the phantasms of the imagination. In the same way, one might ask oneself about the reality of beliefs one has acquired through one's senses or by logical thought. Could one not imagine oneself in a state which compares to being awake, just as wakefulness compares to being asleep? Being awake would be like the dreams of that state, which in turn would show that the illusion (of the certainty) of rational knowledge is nothing but vain imagination.

Such a state might be the one that the mystics (Sufis) claim, for they assert that when they become totally absorbed in themselves and completely abstract from their senses they find themselves in a state of mind which does not agree with what is given by reason.

Perhaps this state is none other than death? Did not Allah's messenger, peace be upon him, say: "Men are asleep; in dying they awaken."[32] Life here below may be a stream, compared with life beyond. After death, things would appear in a different light, and, as the *Qur'ān* says, "We have lifted your veil, and today your sight is penetrating."[33]

When these thoughts came to my mind and gnawed at me I

tried to find some way of treating my unhealthy condition, but this was in vain. They could be dispelled only by reasoning, which is impossible without recourse to the first principles of knowledge. If these are not admissible, no construction of a proof is possible.

My disease grew worse and lasted almost two months, during which I fell prey to skepticism (*safsaṭa*), though neither in theory nor in outward expression. At last, God the Almighty cured me of that disease and I recovered my health and mental equilibrium. The self-evident principles of reason again seemed acceptable; I trusted them and in them felt safe and certain.[34] I reached this point not by well-ordered or methodical argument, but by means of a light God the Almighty cast into my breast,[35] which light is the key to most knowledge.[36]

Anyone who believes that the "unveiling of truth is the fruit of well-ordered arguments belittles the immensity of divine mercy. God's messenger — peace be upon him — was asked about spiritual expansion and the sense in which this is found in the word of God: "Him who when God wishes to direct, He opens his breast to Islam."[37] He said, "It is a light which God the Almighty throws upon the heart." When they asked him, "How may we recognize it?" he replied, "By this, that a person abandons every vanity to return to eternity."[38] Muḥammad — peace be upon him — also said, "God the Almighty created humankind in darkness, and then scattered some of His light upon them."[39] It is to this light that one should look for inspiration. In certain circumstances it springs up from the depths of divine goodness. We must be on the lookout for it, according to the saying of Muḥammad — peace be upon him — "It happens that your Lord sends messages of grace on certain days of your life; be ready for these messages."[40]

To sum up, know that in the quest for truth one must strive for perfection, even to the point of seeking the unseekable. Primary truths have no need of being sought because they are present in the mind. What is present will disappear if you seek it, but one who seeks the unseekable will not be suspected of having been negligent in seeking what can be sought.

CHAPTER II

THE CATEGORIES OF SEEKERS

When God the Almighty had cured me of this disease through His mercy and immense goodness, I perceived that the categories of those who seek (truth) are divided into four groups:

1. The scholastics (*mutakallimūn*), who claim discernment and speculative capabilities.

2. The interiorists (*bāṭiniyya*), who claim to be the masters of teaching (*ta'līm*) and are characterized by their belief in the need for an infallible *Imām*.

3. The philosophers (*Falāsifah*), who consider themselves exponents of logic and proof.

4. The mystics (*ṣūfiyya*), who seek the privilege of Divine Presence (Ahl al-Ḥaḍra), vision and inspiration.[41]

I said then to myself: truth does not escape these four groups of seekers, for they follow the path which leads thereto. Were truth to elude them there would be no hope of ever finding it, especially not by conformism. The conformist is excluded from the beginning for he could succeed in finding the truth only by realizing that he is deceived in being a conformist. Then his glass shield would shatter; the pieces could never be reassembled, but would have to be melted down and recast once again as a new form.

I soon set myself to follow these four paths and to examine what these groups hold, beginning with scholasticism, passing through philosophy and interiorism, and finishing with the mysticism of the Sufis.

PART I

THE SCIENCE OF KALĀM: ITS AIMS AND ACHIEVEMENTS[42]

I began with the study of scholasticism and studied it thoroughly. I read the books written by its well-established scholars and wrote some myself. I discovered it to be a science that served their (the theologian's) own purposes, which, however, were not mine. Its only purpose is to preserve the creed of orthodox (Sunnite) faith and to protect it against the confusion brought by innovators.

God transmitted to His people, by the voice of His Prophet, a creed which is the true faith concerning both this world and the hereafter, as is stated in the *Qur'ān* and the traditions (*Sunna*).[43] Then, through the ideas of the innovators, the devil introduced heresies contrary to the tradition (*Sunna*).[44] Vigorously quoting them, the innovators were on the point of corrupting the true creed for its adherents.

That is when God raised up the scholastics to defend the tradition by a series of well-ordered discourses which revealed the heresies which had been mischievously innovated. That is the origin of scholasticism and its teachers.[45] Some have carried out their task honestly: they have defended the tradition, repulsed the attacks on the faith of the Prophet, and fought against religious innovations.

But in doing this they used arguments borrowed in a spirit of concession from their adversaries. They accepted these either uncritically or based on the consensus of the Muslim nation, or by too simply accepting (a supposed meaning) of the *Qur'ān* and the *Hadīths* (traditions).[46]

Most often their argument was restricted to revealing the contradictions in the opposing view and to attacking their conclusions from their premises. This was not of great use to anyone who does not concede anything beyond the basic certainties. For myself, scholasticism brought little satisfaction and could not cure the sickness from which I suffered.[47]

It is true that after a long time the advocates of *Kalām* wished to defend the tradition by searching deeply into the nature of things. They have undertaken research into substance, accidents and natural laws.[48] But since the purpose of their science lay elsewhere, what they said fell short of its goal. The result has not helped to dissipate the dark confusion due to the differences of opinion among persons.

I do not doubt that others have had a better experience than I, perhaps even a whole category of persons. But for them this was mixed with a blind acceptance of questions which have nothing to do with basic principles. My present goal is to reveal the state of my soul, not in order to blame those who have sought a remedy in scholasticism, for healing medicines vary according to the disease: those which benefit some patients will harm others.

PART II

PHILOSOPHY

On the essence of philosophy: what is blameworthy in it, and what is not; what makes its patron an unbeliever and what does not; what makes one an innovator or heretic and what does not; what philosophers have plagiarized from the works of the people of truth and incorporated into their writings in order to propagate their own falsehoods together with those truths; how souls come to refrain from truth; and how to distinguish unadulterated truth from the falsehood and deceptions found in the philosophers' teaching.[49]

Having finished with scholasticism, I passed over to philosophy (*falsāfah*). I knew very well that it is impossible to detect the distortions in a branch of knowledge without a deep understanding of it rivaling those most knowledgeable in that subject. One must even outstrip them to sound the depths and explore the perils which its teachers had ignored. Only in this way may one hope to expose its weak points. But I do not know any Muslim scholar who has taken up this approach.

The books of the scholastics, in so far as they were concerned to respond to the philosophers, contain nothing but obscure and sparse allusions. They have evident contradictions and errors and do not seem capable of convincing a person of average intelligence, let alone one familiar with the subtleties of the science.

I have learned that to attempt to refute a system without understanding it or knowing it through and through is to do so blindfold. Therefore I set myself to a serious study of this science (of philosophy) through its written works, reading them without the help of a teacher. I did this during leisure moments while working on the composition and teaching of religious law[50] — at this time in Baghdad I had 300 pupils to teach and instruct.

Thank God, reading alone in these stolen moments allowed me to understand the deep secrets of philosophy in less than two years. I continued after this to reflect upon the subject for nearly a year: returning to it, taking it up again, and reexamining its depths and its hidden dangers. Finally I was in a position to sum up with great certainty what it contained of heresy and of both practical and abstract delusions.[51]

Here is my exposé of the philosophers and the results of their sciences. There are many categories of philosophers and many branches of philosophy, but throughout their numerous schools they suffer from the defect of being infidels and irreligious,[52] though among the different groups of philosophers the older seem less distant from the truth than do others.

A. The Categories of Philosophers and Their Atheism

Considering their many groups and their different theories, the philosophers can be divided into three categories: materialists, naturalists and theists:

1. *The materialists (dahriyyūn).*[53] This oldest group denies the existence of the Creator — Ruler, Omniscient and Omnipotent,[54] — maintaining that the universe always has existed by itself without a maker. According to them, the animal issued from the sperm, and the sperm from the animal continuously. These are atheist *(zanād iqa).*[55]

2. *The naturalists (tabī'iyyūn)*[56] have carried out much research into the natural world and the wonders of the animal and vegetable kingdom; they have advanced the anatomical study of animal organisms. What they have seen of the wonders of creation, the works of divine wisdom, has obliged them to acknowledge a wise creator, knowledgeable about things and their ends. It is not possible to study anatomy and the marvelous functioning of the organs without perceiving the necessary perfection of Him who formed the body of the animal, or above all that of human beings.[57]

Nevertheless, the naturalists have concluded on the basis of their research that the balance of one's humors[58] has a great influence on one's physical constitution. They believed further that the faculty of reasoning depended on this, to the extent that the faculty would disappear without this balance. And it seemed inconceivable to them that once it ceased to exist it could be reborn.

Hence, they held that the human soul dies and does not return to life. They denied the Hereafter, Paradise and Hell, Resurrection and Judgment.[59] The reward for good behavior and the punishment of the bad becomes pointless. Unchecked, these naturalists have plunged like animals into lechery. They are also atheists, since faith has to be in God and the Day of Judgment, whereas even if the naturalists believed in God and His attributes, they have denied the existence of the Last Judgment.

3. *The theists* (*ilāhiyyūn*)[60] are the most recent. Among them were Socrates, the teacher of Plato, the teacher of Aristotle. Aristotle put them on a logical footing, systematized the philosophical sciences, developed them and brought their fruit to maturity. In general, the theists refuted the pretensions of the materialists and naturalists and, by exposing their shameful errors, saved others the task. In this way, God saved the believers the trouble of combatting such errors.[61]

At great length and sparing no effort, Aristotle refuted the allegations of Plato, Socrates and those theists who preceded them. He distanced himself from them, although he could not avoid preserving traces of their ugly heresies and innovations. They all should be regarded as heretics, as should their successors: such Muslim, philosophers as Ibn Sīnā (Avicenna)[62] and al-Fārābī,[63] and their like.[64] More than any, these two contributed to the spread of Aristotle's ideas.

The errors and confusions in the work of the other philosophers have so troubled their readers as to appear unintelligible. But how can one reject or accept something that one does not understand? Aristotle's authentic philosophy, if we keep to what al-Fārābī and Avicenna transmitted to us, consisted of three parts: the first two would be condemned, one for disbelief, the other for innovation or heresy (*tabdī*); the third would not be condemned without appeal.[65]

B. The Divisions of the Philosophical Sciences

The sciences that concern the philosophers in relation to our aim are divided into six categories: mathematics, logic, the natural sciences, metaphysics, politics and ethics.

1. *Mathematics*. This deals with arithmetic, geometry and astronomy, but nothing in them relates positively or negatively to religious matters. Mathematics treats demonstrable matters[66] which in no way can be denied once they are known and understood.

However this presents two risks.

The first risk from studying mathematics is that the student is struck by the precision of this science and the imposing power of its proofs. He extends this high esteem to all the philosophical disciplines and attempts to generalize the clarity and firmness had by mathematical proofs. Then, when he hears mathematicians being reproached as heretics, for having negative attitudes[67] or for being scornful of revelation, he rejects the truths which he had admitted previously through pure conformism. If faith were true, he will say to himself, how is it that these mathematical experts have not perceived it? As people say that they are heretics and irreligious, truth must consist in rejecting and denying religious beliefs. How many people have lost their faith because of this simple argument!

The answer is that each technician is a specialist. The lawyer or scholastic is not necessarily a good physician; one who is ignorant of metaphysics is not necessarily ignorant of grammar. Every technique has its unrivalled experts who are ignorant and stupid in other fields. The mathematics of the ancients[68] was founded on proofs, their study of divinity was founded on speculation. But this can be known only to an experienced person who has made a thorough investigation of the matter.

Unfortunately, these considerations escape those whose faith is only a matter of conformism. They persist in having a good opinion of all the philosophical disciplines, driven as they are by vain passions,[69] destructive irony, and the desire to appear clever.

As the risk is considerable, it is fitting to warn regarding mathematics. Although it has no connection with religion, it provides the basis for the other sciences; anyone who studies it risks infection by their vices. Few who study it escape the danger of loss of faith.[70]

The second risk comes from the ignorant, if faithful, Muslim. Imagining that one should defend one's faith by rejecting all philosophy, such a one rejects all the sciences, going so far as to deny the scientific explanations for eclipses of the sun or the moon, claiming that they contradict Islam.[71] If this reaches the ears of someone who has learned about necessary truths, he will not begin to doubt the scientific explanations, but will doubt the basis of Islam, believing it to be founded upon ignorance and a denial of truth. This can do nothing but consolidate a person's love for philosophy and hatred of

Islam. People who imagine that they are defending Islam when they reject the philosophical sciences are really doing great harm to Islam. It assumes[72] neither a positive nor a negative attitude to such sciences, which in no way are opposed to religion.

The prophet Muḥammad — peace be upon him — has said: "The sun and the moon are two of the divine signs. They are eclipsed neither for the death nor for the birth of anyone. When you see an eclipse you should have recourse to praise of God and prayer."[73] Where in these words is there mention of any rejection of arithmetic,[74] which calculates in a particular way the path of the sun and the moon, their conjunction and their opposition?

As for the prophet's saying: "But when God reveals Himself to something it humbles itself before Him", this addition is not found in the authenticated collections of *Hadīths*.[75] Those are the two risks which mathematics can present.

2. *Logic*. This science has nothing to do with faith, which it neither approves nor disapproves. It is restricted to an examination of methods of demonstration, syllogisms and reasoning by analogy; to the conditions of the premises of proof and the modes of their combination; and to the conditions of exact definition and how it is to be drawn up. Logic is concerned solely with the concept, which is a question of definition, and with judging the truth of something,[76] which is a question of proof.

There is nothing in that which should be rejected. Scholastic and speculative scholars[77] already have made use of it. The logicians differ from them only in their vocabulary, their terminology, their definitions and their more profound classifications. Here is an example of their reasoning: "If one admits that all A is B, it must follow that some B is also A. In other words, if it is true that all humans are animals, it must follow that some animals are men." This is what they mean when they say that a universal truth is the reverse of a partial truth.

What connection is there between such logic and religious questions, which would require one to reject or condemn it? If you condemned it you would gain a poor reputation among the logicians, first for your own poor mind, but above all for the religion which you claim to be founded apparently on this denial.

It is true that there is some injustice on the part of logicians. They wish to accumulate for their proofs conditions they know to be capable of giving rise to infallible certainty, about which there can be no doubt. But when they take up questions of religion, they cannot realize these conditions and do not follow their own principles. Thus, someone who admires logic will imagine that the blasphemies attributed to the philosophers are based on seemingly solid proofs and quickly will opt for a heresy before even having studied theodicy. Thus, logic too[78] is not without risks.

3. *The Natural Sciences.* These deal with the heavens and the stars, as well as with such simple bodies below as water, air, earth, fire, and such organic bodies as animals, vegetables and minerals. They examine also the causes of their change, transformations and mixtures. They proceed like medicine in its study of the anatomy of the parts of the body and the causes of the mixing of humors. It is no more necessary for religion to reject the natural sciences than the science of medicine, except for a few points mentioned in our book on *The Incoherence of the Philosophers* (*Tahāfut*[79]*al Falāsifah*). The other points of disagreement are subsumed in these.

The basic theme of these natural sciences is to recognize that all nature is in the service of the All-powerful; nature does not act of itself, but is used in the service of the Creator. It is thus that the sun, the moon, the stars and the elements are subject to God's command. Nothing in them is able to act independently by and of itself.[80]

4. *Metaphysics.* This contains most of the philosophers' errors. Because these scholars are not able to furnish the proofs which their logic requires, they contradict each other in this domain. On this point, Aristotle's theory is close to that of Muslims as regards what is transmitted by al-Fārābī and Ibn Sīnā. But the sum of their errors amounts to twenty basic articles,[81] all of which would excommunicate the philosophers: three count as heresy, and the other seventeen as innovations. To refute these twenty errors I wrote *al-Tahāfut* (*The Incoherence of the Philosophers*).

Here, to start with, are the three main heresies, which have excommunicated their holders from Islam:

a. They hold that at the Last Judgment human bodies will not be reassembled[82] but the souls alone will be rewarded or punished. They also say that the rewards and punishments will be spiritual, not physical. They are right to insist on the spiritual rewards and punishments, which in itself is certain. But they are wrong to deny the physical rewards and punishments. This is a sheer denial of the revealed law.

b. They also believe that God knows the universal but not the particular, which is also a proper heresy; what is correct is that, "In heaven as on earth, not an atom escapes His knowledge."[83]

c. They affirm further the preexistence of the universe and its eternity,[84] something that no Muslim has ever believed.[85] On other questions — such as the denial of the Attributes of God, and maintaining that God knows through His essence rather than by knowledge added thereto, and similar ideas — their doctrine is close to the theories of the Mu'tazilites.[86] But they should not be considered heretical on the basis of such views. In my work, "The Clear Criterion for Distinguishing between Islam and Godlessness",[87] I mentioned that, as well as the error of those who are quick to condemn as heresy anything not of their own system.

5. *Politics*. On the whole, politics concerns the management of temporal government and the authority of rulers. It has taken its maxims from the Books revealed by God to the prophets, and the maxims of the ancient prophets.[88]

6. *Ethics*. The object of the science of ethics comes down to the study of the qualities of the soul and of character, their different categories, and the way to cultivate and direct them. The moralists took their doctrine from the mystics (Sufis).[89] These are holy men who devote themselves to calling upon God[90] the Almighty, to struggling against the passions, and to following the divine path, while separating themselves from the good things of this world. In their spiritual states, human nature and its faults and vices have been revealed to them: they have explained this clearly.

The philosophers took over what the mystics said, and incorporated it into their own teaching in order to spread their errors under the bright luster of the mystics. In their time, as always, there was one of those groups which God never leaves the world without, for they are the pillars which support the earth.[91] God's mercy descends upon it because of their spirit, in accord with Muḥammad's saying — peace be upon him — "It is by them that the rain and your subsistence comes to you." The sleepers in the cave[92] were of such persons. According to the *Qur'ān* there were such persons in ancient times.

C. The Dangers of Philosophy

The philosophers have incorporated in their writings the sayings of the prophets and the maxims of the mystics. From this there has arisen a double risk, both for the one who accepts their teachings and for the one who rejects them.

1. *The danger of rejecting philosophy is considerable.* Some weak spirits have believed that they should reject the words of the prophets and mystics because these are found among erroneous statements in the writings of the philosophers. They even thought they should not cite these as extracted from the philosophers, because, to their weak minds, such sayings would be false because uttered by those in error.

This attitude is like that of people who criticize Christians for saying, "There is no god but God, and Jesus is the messenger of God." They say, that is what the Christians say, without stopping to think whether the Christian is an unbeliever because of this saying, or because of his denial of Muḥammad as a Prophet — peace be upon him. If one is an unbeliever only because of what he denies, he should not be opposed in anything other than what he denies of the things which are inherently true, even though the Christian also holds it to be such. That is the mistake made by people of weak minds: they do not recognize the truth except in the mouth of certain people, instead of recognizing people when they speak the truth.

On the contrary, a wise man follows the advice of the commander of believers, 'Alī Ibn Abū Ṭālib,[93] who said, "Do not recognize the truth in the mouth of certain men, but first recognize the truth and then you will recognize who are truthful." An initiate, a wise man, begins by recognizing what is true and after that examines individual sayings. If one of these is truthful, he accepts it, whether the person who said it is in error or in truth.

A wise person may even attempt to isolate the part of the truth which is contained in the statements of mistaken people. He is well aware that grains of gold are hidden in the sand and that the experienced money-changer takes no risk in hunting through a forger's[94] moneybag in order to separate the pure gold from the false coins. Of course, one would not allow a rustic to deal with a forger:

one keeps the fool away from the riverbank, but not the expert swimmer; one forbids the child to touch the snake, but there is no danger for the snake-charmer.

Alas, most people are too quick to believe themselves capable, expert and perfectly capable intellectually to discriminate between the true and the false, between the straight path and error. Hence, it would be better if it were possible to forbid everyone from reading the writings of mistaken people, so that those who might escape the danger of rejecting philosophy might also avoid accepting it *en bloc*.

On the other hand, some of my readers have criticized some passages of my books dealing with the mysteries of religion. They have not studied the sciences sufficiently deeply, and their minds have not been able to embrace the full implications of our teachings. They believed that those passages were borrowed from the ancient philosophers. In fact, some of my expressions were the fruit of my own thinking (and why should the tracks of one horse not cover those of another); some of them can be found in the sacred texts; many others are to be found, in substance, in the works of the mystics.

But even if my words could be found nowhere but in the writings of the ancient philosophers, why should they be dismissed, if they are acceptable, demonstrable, and in accord with the *Qur'ān* and the traditions? If we were to open this door and begin to reject every truth that has already been discovered by a mistaken author, we would have to reject a great deal, including the Qur'ānic verses, sayings of the Prophet, narratives of the ancients, and sayings of the wise men and the mystics. It would be enough to argue that they had been quoted by the author of the book of the Brethren of Purity[95] who used them as a basis for his argument and to deceive his stupid readers. Mistaken thinkers borrow from us authentic quotations and introduce them into their writings.

Nevertheless, the least that one should require of a scholar is that he should be distinguishable from the ignorant common man: he knows that honey keeps its flavor, even if contained in the cup of one who lets blood, for he knows well that the substance of honey does not change according to its recipient. His natural revulsion is due to ignorance, to the fact that the cup is made to receive blood deemed inpure;[96] but it is not the cup that makes the blood dirty, the blood is already dirty. Honey is nothing of the sort and is not spoiled by being in the bloodletter's cup.

Nevertheless this sort of error is common. Most people will agree with a statement, even if false, provided it is believed by someone they admire; whereas they reject it, even if true, when it comes from the mouth of people they do not like. This is equivalent to judging truth according to who speaks it, instead of judging people according to whether or not they speak the truth. This is enough about the danger of rejecting philosophy.

2. *The danger of accepting philosophy* is that one who studies books, such as those of the Brethren of Purity and others, sees that they are full of tasty bits taken from the sayings of the prophets and maxims of the mystics. It is possible to appreciate and agree with them, but this would be tantamount to accepting the error of their teaching under the pretext of preserving the partial truth that it contains. Because of this danger, we have to forbid reading them. This essential precaution is like the prudence of keeping non-swimmers away from the sea, and keeping children away from snakes.

A snake-charmer should not manipulate snakes in the presence of his small child, who might want to imitate his father's actions, thinking to be like his father. The child should be warned by the example of his father in not touching the snake in front of him. The scholar who is firm in knowledge should do the same.

On the other hand, the expert snake-charmer grabs hold of the snake, chooses between the venom and the antidote, extracts the antidote from the glands and overcomes the venom: he must not refuse the antidote to anyone who has need of it. In the same way, the observant money-changer searches the bag of the forger and separates the pure gold from the counterfeits: he too must not refuse gold to anyone who asks him for it.

Also it is necessary to overcome the repugnance of a sick person for the antidote which he knows to have been taken from a poisonous snake. It is also necessary to explain to a poor person, who does not dare draw on the purse of the forger, that he risks falling victim to his ignorance. He must be made to understand that truth and error do not contaminate each other, and above all that they do not change their meaning from the simple fact of being side by side. That is all I wish to say about the dangers which philosophy may present.

PART III

THE THEOLOGY OF TEACHING (*TA'LĪM*)[97] AND THE DANGERS WHICH ARISE THEREFROM

When I had finished with philosophy, having examined it well and revealed its error, I perceived how inadequate was this science, for reason alone cannot clear up every problem and resolve every difficulty.

After that, there came on the scene the supporters of teaching (*Ta'līm*), who spread theories about the acquisition of knowledge via the intermediary of an infallible Imām or teacher of the truth.

I was about to start studying their doctrine and to read their books[98] when a formal order from his Highness, the Caliph, obliged me to write a treatise on this subject to disclose their true themes.[99] As I could not avoid this, my personal impulse was now given an external motivation. Therefore I began to collect the texts and the sayings attributed to supporters of "education" or teaching; I took account of recent discussions, which differed from the opinions of the first representatives of the sect. In this way I assembled a well-ordered collection, and dressed a complete reply, to such an extent, indeed, that certain "People of the Truth"[100] then reproached me for my favorable attitude. They said, "You have done their work! Without you, your detailed study, and the logic of your exposé, they would never have been able to know the precise flow of their thought."

This reproach is not without foundation. When Aḥmad Ibn Hanbal[101] criticized al-Ḥārith al-Muhāsibī[102] — may Allah be pleased with them — for his attacks on the Mu'tazila, al-Ḥārith replied that "It is obligatory to refute innovation." But Aḥmad replied, "Indeed, but you have begun by quoting their uncertainties, before replying to them. How do you know that one of your readers will not absorb the uncertainties without taking note of your reply, or read your reply without really understanding it?"

This remark by Aḥmad is just, on condition that it is a question of an uncertainty, of something equivocal which is not already widely known. Otherwise it is quite necessary to answer it, which is to begin by exposing it.

Of course, it would be useless to speak of an equivocal thought that the supporters of "education" have never held. I have not done this. But one of my friends, who used to be one of them suggested this. He told me that the sect in question laughs at its detractors' works, saying that they have understood nothing of their position. It was then that he explained to me what they do believe. I reviewed it later so as not to be accused of ignorance; I made a clear exposé of it so that no one could accuse me of not having understood any of it. I even pushed it to the absurd, in order to make apodictic proof of its errors.

The result of all this was to reveal that this group has nothing of value to offer. This innovation, so weak in content, would not have made such an uproar without the help of the ignorant friends of truth. But their passion for the truth has led the defenders of the faith to have long discussions with this group, in order to condemn their theories, namely, the "necessity of teaching dispensed by a teacher", and "not just any teacher suffices; it must be an infallible teacher."

This double thesis, the need of authoritative teaching and the infallible teacher has had wide circulation, while the arguments against it have appeared weak. Some people have even believed in the solid basis of "teaching" and the weakness of its adversaries, instead of perceiving the ignorance of the former.

It is true that we need a teacher, an infallible master, but he already exists. This is the Prophet Muḥammad — peace be upon him.

Should they say, but he is dead, we shall answer: your teacher is in hiding.

If they say, our teacher has trained and sent out missionaries; he is awaiting their return in order to enquire about their disagreements and problems, we shall reply that our master also trained and sent out missionaries, and that his teaching is perfect, for God the Almighty said, "Today I perfected your religion and gave you my entire benefaction."[103] Since that time, the teaching has been complete; the death or absence of the teacher cannot affect it.

There remains one question: "How can one judge something

on which one has not been instructed? Is it by reference to a text that has not been taught? Or by making an effort at personal interpretation *(Ijtihād)*[104] and discernment, which presume disagreement?"[105] Here is the answer: "Do as Mu'ādh did, when the Prophet — peace be upon him — sent him to the Yemen: we use the text, if it exists; if not, then personal judgment."[106]

Thus, we shall imitate the propagandists of "teaching", doing what they do when they are far from their Imām. With limited texts they cannot make decisions on an infinite number of cases. Nor can they travel to consult their Imām, and then travel back to the person who consulted them. The person surely would have died in the meantime, so that the return would be useless.

For a person who is not sure of the direction of the Kibla,[107] all he can do is trust his own judgment. If he took the time to go to consult the Imām, he would miss the hour of prayer. Thus, it is permitted to pray in the direction one estimates to be true, though it may not be the real direction of Macca. Indeed, it has been said, "He who is mistaken in his personal judgment deserves a reward, while he who judges correctly deserves a double reward." Everything that depends on an effort of personal interpretation is of this sort. For example, for legal almsgiving[108] the recipient may be poor in the personal judgment of the donor, whereas secretly he is wealthy. This mistake is not sinful because it was based on conjecture.

One may say, "My adversary's opinion is as good as mine." We reply, "He is obliged to follow his own opinion, like the person who trusts his own judgment about the direction of prayer, even if the others do not agree."

Should one ask whether "the conformist must follow Abū Hanīfa,[109] or al-Shāfi'ī[110] — God be pleased with them both — or others, I reply, "If a person relies on conformism when he is in doubt about the direction of Macca, what will he do if the initiated disagree?" One will say that he must choose from among them the best qualified and most knowledgeable about the direction of the Kibla, and then follow personal judgement in this particular domain. It is the same as regards the different schools of thought.[111]

In this way the Prophet and religious leaders were forced to refer the faithful to personal interpretation, despite the risk of error. The Prophet — peace be upon him — said, "I judge by appearances, it is God who looks after what is hidden."[112] This means, "I judge according to general opinion taken from fallible witnesses, though they may be mistaken." If the prophets themselves were not immune to error in matters of personal judgement, how much more so ourselves?

There are two obvious objections here:

The first is that this attitude is permitted in the case of personal thinking, but cannot apply to the very basis of the faith:[113] one who makes a mistake there cannot be pardoned, how can one answer that? The answer is that: "The basis of the faith is found in the *Qur'ān* and in the tradition. For the remaining details or disagreements, the truth can be determined by recourse to the just balance, that is, to the collection of five rules — cited in the Book and recalled in my treatise, *The Just Balance*."[114]

Objection: "This criterion is not recognized by your adversaries." Reply: "If completely understood, it is inconceivable that anyone could fail to recognize it. How could supporters of teaching disagree about it, for I took it from the *Qur'ān* and learned it from the same Book.[115] The logicians do not disagree for it agrees completely with the conditions and rules of logic. Nor will the scholastics disagree, for it agrees with their ideas about speculative demonstrations and the criterion of truth in the scholastic domain."

Objection: "If you possess such a criterion, why have you not put an end to all disagreement among people?" Reply: "I would do so if they would listen to me. In my treatise, *The Just Balance*, I have explained this. Reflect and you will see that my criterion is good and would suppress all discord if people would only listen to it. But not everyone will listen. Those who have, I have led to agree. Further, your Imām[116] wants them all to be in accord, although they do not listen much; why has he not managed yet to achieve this agreement?"

"Why did Ali — God be pleased with him — the first of the Imāms, fail? Did he think he could make them docile in spite of themselves? Why has he failed so far; till what point has he postponed success; what result has he had except to increase discord and the number of his adversaries? Yes, it is to be feared that this discord might lead to bloodshed, devastation, the orphaning of children, brigandage and pillage. Across the world, your work of pacification so far has brought unheard of disagreement."

If one says: "You wish to put an end to all discord, but any-one hesitating between opposing schools and rival sects[117] will not want to hear only your side, and not that of your adversary. Most of them are against you, and one cannot see any difference between you and them." This is their second objection. I reply: "This objection above all recoils upon your own head. It is true that the puzzled reader you wish to attract might ask you what makes you better than the others, when most men of science are in disagreement with you. I should like to know what you would say? Should you say, 'My Imām is indicated by a text,'[118] who would believe you, for this text has not come from the mouth of the prophets. The men of science agree about your inventions and your falsehoods."

However, suppose we admit that the puzzled reader concedes that you possess this text, but doubts the basis of the prophethood. He suggests that your Imām have recourse to the miracle wrought by Jesus, saying, "The proof of my authenticity is that I resurrect your father." But suppose he does resurrect him, people did not all agree on the authenticity of Jesus because he performed such a miracle.[119]

"Indeed, in this field there are problems which can be re-solved only by detailed reasoning. According to you, however, reasoning cannot be trusted. Yet a miracle does not prove authentic-ity (unless one knows what magic is and can distinguish between magic and miracle). One needs to know also whether God ever misleads His servants — a delicate but familiar question.[120] What then could you answer, for your Imām has no more right to be fol-lowed than have his detractors."

The supporters of teaching reject the rational arguments their adversaries present, or even clearer ones. Thus, this second objec-tion has very badly turned against its authors: from the first to the last, none is able to answer them.

The spread of error has been the fault of weak persons who wanted to reason with them. Instead of arguing rationally, they only made retorts which prolong the debate but do not save time or si-lence the adversary.

Should one say, "This is an argument by retort, but is there a direct reply?" I answer, "Yes. One who says he is puzzled without specifying what he is puzzled about is like a sick person who asks for a cure for his illness without saying what it is." The latter should be told that there is no cure for illness in general, but only for a particular malady, such as migraine, diarrhoea or their like. The questioner must describe his difficulty. Then one shows him how to apply my five rules. If he understands them, he will recognize that they contain the norm of truth, an accurate measure, and the criterion of precise thought. Thus, someone who is studying arithmetic will understand simultaneously the calculation and the authentic scientific knowledge of the teacher. I have explained all this clearly in about twenty pages in my treatise *The Just Balance*, which should be studied.

My actual intent is not to reveal the error of their doctrine. I have already done so in my earlier works: first, *al-Mustazhirī*; secondly, the book *Kitāb hujjat al-ḥaqq* which replies to ideas from Baghdad; thirdly, the book *Mifsal al-khilāf*, in twelve chapters, where I reply to ideas gathered in Hamadhān; fourthly, the book *al-Darj al-Marqūm*, arranged in tables, which contains some mediocre ideas of theirs collected in Tūs; and fifthly, in the book *al-Qisṭās al-Mustaqīm* (*The Just Balance*), an independent book directed at exposing the criteria of the sciences and showing that one can do without an infallible Imām. Here I will restrict myself to bringing out that these men offer no remedy at all to the different obscure opinions.

In spite of their inability to prove the designation of the Imām, we long agreed with them. We shared their conviction on the need for teaching and for an infallible teacher. But to our questions on this teaching and the problems we put to them, they were not able to understand, let alone to reply. When they failed they referred us to the hidden Imām, saying, "It is absolutely necessary to go to see him." It is astonishing that they waste their life in seeking after the Imām and arrogantly claim to have found him, but strangely have not learned anything from him. They are like a dirty person who wears himself out looking for water, but does not wash himself when he finds it, and thus remains dirty.

A certain number of them claims to know a little of the teaching, which amounts to a few insipid crumbs of Pythagoras's philosophy. He was one of the early ancient thinkers, and his doctrine is even more weak than that of the philosophers. Aristotle refuted it and revealed the weakness and error of his theories, yet this can be found once again in the book of the Brethren of Purity; it is the refuse of philosophy.

It is strange to see these people struggling all their lives in search of knowledge, only to be content with worthless banalities while believing they have reached the highest point of knowledge. We have kept in touch with them, and have sounded out their exterior and interior semblance of truth. Their efforts are limited to making the common people and weak minds gradually admit the need to go to a teacher. If one refuses, they begin to argue harshly in order to silence him. If one agrees and asks to learn the science of the teacher in order to profit from it, they stop and say, "Because you admit this, go and search out the teacher yourself." They know full well that if they go further they will be covered in shame, since they are incapable of resolving the least difficulty, or even understanding it, let alone replying to it.

That is what they are like. Once you try them, you will hate them.[121] We have kept company with them, but now have washed our hands of them.

CHAPTER III

THE MYSTIC WAYS
(*ṢŪFĪYYA*)

After I had finished with those branches of knowledge, I directed my mind entirely to the Way of the mystics. I came to know that their Way[122] consists of both knowledge and deeds as equally necessary. The object of their works[123] is to eliminate the obstacles created by one's own self,[124] and to eradicate the defects and vices in one's own character. In this way, in the end the heart will get rid of all that is not God the Almighty, and will adorn itself solely with praise of God.

However, I found that knowledge came more easily to me than deeds. Therefore, I began to learn their teaching by reading their mystic works, such as *Qūt al-qulūb* ("Food of Hearts"), by Abū Ṭālib al-Makkī[125] — God be pleased with him — the works of al-Harith al-Muhāsibī,[126] and the quotations from a l Junayd,[127] al-Shiblī[128] and Abū Yazid al-Bistāmī[129] and the sayings of other sheikhs — God hallow their spirits.

By doing this I learned the essence of their theoretical thinking and as much as can be learned through teaching and listening.

But it became clear to me that what is proper to it can be learnt only through savoring or experiencing[130] the mystic states of the soul,[131] and the exchange of attributes (or behavioral attitudes).[132] With regard to health and satisfaction, consider what a difference there is between, on the one hand, simple knowledge of their respective definitions, causes and conditions, and, on the other hand, the reality of being oneself in good health or satisfied, or between the reality of being drunk and academic knowledge of the definition of drunkenness as the state caused by vapors rising from the stomach to the brain. A drunkard does not know the definition or scientific explanation of drunkenness: he does not even worry his head about it.[133] But a physician[134] knows them perfectly, without experiencing drunkenness in reality. In the same way, a sick physician may know the definition of health, its causes, and the remedies which will re-establish it, but still he is ill. Thus, it is one thing to know all about the ascetic life, its conditions and causes, but something completely different to be effectively in an ascetic state of soul, completely detached from the good things of this world.

I became certain that the mystics are not great as speech makers,[135] but that they do achieve certain states of soul. I learned what could be learned; the rest comes only from experience and following the path oneself.[136] As a result of my research in the field of both religious and rational sciences, I have already arrived at an unshakable faith in God, in prophethood, and in the Last Judgment. These three principles of religion were engraved deeply in my heart, not because of carefully elaborated argument, but as a result of particular reasons, circumstances and experiences, too many to be listed here in detail.[137]

I also perceived that I could not hope for eternal happiness unless I feared God and rejected all the passions, that is to say, I should begin by breaking my heart's attachment to the world. I needed to abandon the illusions of life on earth in order to direct my attention towards my eternal home with the most intense desire for God, the Almighty. This entailed avoiding all honors and wealth, and escaping from everything that usually occupies a person and ties him down.

Turning to look inward, I perceived that I was bound by attachments on all sides. I meditated on all that I had done, teaching and instructing being my proudest achievements, and I perceived that all my studies were futile, since they were of no value for the Way to the hereafter.[138] Moreover, what had been my purpose in teaching? My intention had not been pure, for it had not been directed towards God the Almighty alone. Had I not preferred to seek glory and renown? I was teetering on the edge of a precipice, and if I did not step back I would plunge into the Fire.

I thought of nothing else, all the time remaining undecided. One day, I would determine to leave Baghdad and lead a new life, but the next day I would change my mind. I took one step forward, and then one step back. In the morning I might have a desperate thirst for the Hereafter, but by the evening the troops of desire would have stormed and defeated it.

My passions kept me chained in place, while the herald of faith cried, "Take to the road! Take to the road! Life is brief, the journey is long. Knowledge and deeds are nothing but mere outward appearance and illusion.[139] If you are not ready at this very moment for the life to come when will you be ready? And if now you do not break your moorings, when will you break away?" At that moment, I felt impelled to go; my decision to depart and escape would be made.

But Satan returned, saying, "This is only a passing mood! Do not be taken in by it, the feeling will pass quickly. . . . If you give way to it, you will lose your honors, your well-established peaceful and secure position which you will find nowhere else. You will be taking the risk that you will change your mind again and live to regret it. It will not be easy to come back, once you have lost your position. . . ."

This tug of war between my emotions and the summons from the Hereafter lasted nearly six months, from the month of Rajab 488 A.H. (July 1095 A.D.), during which I lost my free will and was under compulsion.

The fact is that God tied my tongue and stopped me teaching. I struggled to no avail to speak at least once to my pupils, to please the hearts of those who were attending my lectures, but my tongue refused to serve me at all. And having my tongue tied made my heart grow heavy. I could not swallow anything; I had no appetite for food or drink; I could neither swallow easily nor digest any solid food.

I grew weak. The physicians despaired of treating me. They said, "The malady has descended to the heart, and has spread from there to the humors. There is no other remedy but to free him from the anxiety which is gnawing at him."[140]

Feeling my impotence, my inability to come to a decision, I put myself in the Hands of God, the ultimate refuge of all those who are in need. I was heard by the One who hears those in need when they pray to Him.[141] He made it easy for me to renounce honors, wealth, family and friends.

I pretended that I planned to travel to Macca, when really I was preparing to leave for Damascus. Actually, I was afraid of alerting the Caliph and some of my friends. Once I had decided never to return, I had to use subterfuges to leave Baghdad. In this way I left myself open to the reproach of the Irāqī scholars, none of whom could imagine that religious motives could lead me to renounce teaching, which they regarded as the summit of religion, for their ideas of the highest knowledge extended no further.[142]

Then, people became entangled in their own hypotheses about

the reasons for my actions. Some, outside Iraq, thought the authorities had insisted on my departure; others, more in touch with Baghdad, seeing that the authorities were trying to keep me whereas I was insisting on leaving, said, "It is a blow from heaven; an evil eye has struck down the Muslims and the wise!"[143]

Those were the circumstances in which I left Baghdad, after distributing my money and keeping only the absolute minimum to feed my children. My Irāqī money was put to good works, invested in pious foundations for Muslims. Nowhere in the world have I seen a better thing that a scholar could do for his family.

I travelled to Damascus, where I spent nearly two years, which I devoted to retreat and solitude, exercises and spiritual combat. I devoted myself entirely to purifying my soul, cleansing my character, and making my heart ready to glorify God the Almighty according to the teachings of the mystics. I spent some time in the mosque in Damascus, passing the entire day from dawn to dusk at the top of the minaret where I shut myself in.[144]

From Damascus I traveled to Jerusalem, where every day I shut myself in the Dome of the Rock.[145] Then I received the call to perform the prescribed pilgrimage to receive the holy blessings of Macca and Medina and to visit the shrine of the Prophet of God — peace be upon him — after having visited the tomb of Abrahām — the friend of God,[146] peace be upon him. I set out on the road for the Hijaz.[147]

Later, certain preoccupations and the appeals of my children summoned me home to my own country. I returned — I, the person least likely to return, who preferred retreat and who had a taste for solitude and a desire to open my heart to prayer. Nevertheless, circumstances, domestic cares and material obligations reversed my decision and interrupted the best part of my solitude, my soul was only intermittently in a state of perfect peace. Nevertheless, I did not cease to aspire thereto, and returned to the attempt again and again, despite every obstacle.

My period of retreat had lasted about ten years,[148] during which I had innumerable inexhaustible revelations. It will be enough to say that the mystic Sufi follow to an uncommon degree the Way of God. Their behavior is perfect, their Way is straight, their character is virtuous. If to this were added the good sense of the reasonable, the wisdom of the wise, and the knowledge of the doctors of law, could one be sure that this would improve their behavior or character? Surely not! Every action or state of theirs, their outward appearance and their inward conscience, is illuminated by the flame of prophecy sitting in its niche[149] beyond which there is no other light on the face of the earth.

What can be said about such a Way? Its purification consists above all of cleansing the heart of everything which is not God, the Almighty. This begins, not with the state of *sacralization* which opens prayer,[150] but by the fusion of the heart with God's Name, and is completed by the total annihilation of the self in God.[151]

Even this is only the first step with regard to one's free will and all that one has learned. It is the first step on the Way itself. What went before[152] was only the waiting room.

Once one has started on the way, one begins to receive inspirations and visions. The mystics keep vigils in which they even see angels and the spirits of the prophets. They hear their voices and have the benefit of their counselling. From these visions of images and symbols they ascend further to degrees of spirituality which cannot be described. Nobody can attempt to express these states of the soul without failing miserably.

In a word, the mystics achieve a nearness to God which some consider to be a virtual in-dwelling,[153] total union,[154] or fusion[155] with God. However, in this they are not correct, as we have shown in our treatise *al Maqsad al-asnā* (*The Greatest Goal*). A person in such a state should say nothing but these lines:[156] "Whatever has ha ppened, I shall not speak of it. Think well about this. Do not question me about it."

In general terms people who have not been privileged to taste this mystical union know nothing of the reality of prophecy, but only its name. The prophets were prefigured (or prepared) by the miracles (or charisma)[157] of the saints.[158] Thus, the first step of Muhammad as a prophet came when he went to pray alone on mount Hirā,[159] and the Arabs said, "Muhammad is burning with longing for God."[160]

Anyone who practices that Way will experience similar states of ecstasy. One who has not experienced them, by keeping company with the mystics, may hear accounts of their experiences and be convinced through the circumstances (of their ecstatic states). Or one may attend their meetings and profit from their belief, for their companions are never in distress.[161]

As for a person who has not been divinely favored to attend their meetings, he may be sure that all this is absolutely proven as I did in the chapter "'Ajā'ib al-Qalb" ("The Wonders of the Heart") in my work, *The Revivification of the Religious Sciences*.[162]

Science[163] is verification by proof; experience or savoring[164] is the intimate knowledge of ecstasy; faith,[165] founded on conjecture, is the acceptance of oral testimony and the evidence of those who have experienced. These are three degrees, and God will raise through this hierarchy those among you who believe and receive the knowledge.[166]

Besides these categories of men, there are the ignorant who in principle deny everything. One speaks to them on this subject; they marvel, listen again, and laugh at it saying "What a story; how he goes on!" It is of these people that God was speaking when He said, "Among unbelievers, some listen to you, but when they go away they ask those who have been given knowledge: what was he going on about just now? They are the people whose hearts have been sealed shut by God and follow pernicious doctrines." "Such are the men whom God has cursed, for He has made them deaf and blinded their eyes."[167]

Having spoken about the mystics; it is necessary to deal with the reality and particular character of prophecy,[168] a completely indispensable matter.

CHAPTER IV

THE TRUE NATURE OF PROPHECY AS A UNIVERSAL HUMAN NEED

Human beings were created originally[169] with an empty and simple mind, unaware that God has other worlds known only to Him. "No one knows the armies of the Lord, save He alone."[170] Man comes to know the world only through his senses, formed to provide him with contact with the world and its different sorts of creatures.

The first sense is that of touch, by which one can feel, for example, hot and cold, wet and dry, smooth and rough, etc. But with this sense alone one could not experience colors or sounds, which do not exist so far as touch is concerned. Next is the sense of sight, which allows one to perceive colors and shapes. It is the most extensive of the sensible worlds. Then comes[171] hearing, which allows one to hear sounds and melodies.[172] Next comes the sense of taste.

At the age of seven years, one reaches the age of discernment and passes beyond the frontiers of the world of senses. One has reached a new stage where one can perceive new things unknown to the senses.

Then one proceeds to another stage, that of intelligence, at which one is able to appreciate what is necessary, what is possible, what is impossible,[173] and things which he could not understand during the earlier stages.

After the stage of intelligence, there comes another realm, a new faculty,[174] which permits him to see hidden things, future events, and many other things which are as unknown to the intellect as is intellect to childish discernment, and as childish understanding, in turn, is to the world of senses.

When confronted with things intelligible to the intellect, a person who has reached only the age of childish discernment will balk and call them improbable. In the same way, certain people who have remained at the stage of intellect have rejected as improbable what they have heard about prophecies. This attitude is pure ignorance, for not having reached the suprarational stage (which does not exist for them personally) these skeptics conclude that it does not exist for anyone. If someone had been born blind and never heard of colors or shapes, but then suddenly heard of them, he would not at all understand what they were and would not believe in them.

In order to make it possible to understand such difficult things, God has given His creatures in the experience of sleep[175] an example of prophecy. A sleeper may have dreams of what will happen, sometimes clear in meaning, sometimes symbolic, which can be explained by interpretation. If someone had never had any personal experience of sleep and it was described to him — some people become lethargic or unconscious, lose their sense of hearing and their sense of sight, and then see things which are hidden — he would say that this was beyond belief and would justify his skepticism by saying, "We perceive things by means of the senses. If someone does not see certain things when he is awake, how will he see them when he is asleep. It is impossible." Yet we have experienced sleep and dreams, so we know that in fact this apparently logical argument by analogy is not valid.

In human life, the intelligence is only one stage in which a person gains a new faculty of perception which allows him to take in all kinds of rational knowledge and things unknown to the realm of the senses. It is similar with prophets, who have, as it were, an extra eye which can perceive things which are invisible and beyond rational understanding.[176] Some people doubt the possibility of prophecy, or doubt its existence, or its realization in a given person. The fact that it exists answers the first doubt whether it is possible. Moreover, everyone knows that there are more things than can be understood by the intellect alone. This is the case in medicine and astronomy.[177] One who studies either of these soon sees that he needs the help of inspiration and guidance from God the Almighty, and that he cannot gain this knowledge from his own experience! There are laws in astronomy that are verifiable only once every thousand years; how could one verify these personally? It is similar with the properties of medicines.

This shows that there are ways of knowing these phenomena in addition to perceiving them with one's own intellect, and that is precisely what prophecy is. But knowledge of things unknowable to the intellect is only one of the numerous aspects of prophecy, only one drop from its ocean. I mention this aspect because I was using the example of dreams, and I mentioned two analogous cases: medicine and astronomy, which enable us to accept the miracles of the prophets which are equally beyond the grasp of the intellect.[178]

As for the other aspects of prophecy, these can be perceived only by suprarational experience[179] had through following the mystic way. Knowledge beyond the grasp of the intellect could be explained to you only by using the example of sleep. How could one believe in other aspects of prophecy if one has no personal experience with which to compare them, for no one will assent to anything until one understands what it is.

In the case of prophecy, it is necessary to set out on the mystic Way, for one attains some first sense of its suprarational capability by exercising it; the result is based on the analogy with what has been attained[180] in assent to things that are beyond logical argument. The fact of that unique unprovable quality of prophecy should make one believe in the principle of prophecy.

Should you doubt the divine inspiration of this or that particular prophet, the solution is to examine his powers, either from your personal experience, or from authentic tradition and hearsay. When you embark on a study of medicine or jurisprudence, for example, you have some idea of doctors and lawyers;[181] you hear them speak, even if you do not know them personally. Nothing prevents you from knowing that al-Shāfi'ī[182] — God be pleased with him — was a jurist, or that Galen[183] was a physician, and knowing this in actual fact, not because someone orders you to believe it. It is sufficient to study a little jurisprudence and medicine and to read the works of these two authors in order to know how they thought.

In the same way, if you have come to understand what prophecy is and if you often read the *Qur'ān* and the tradition you will realize with great certainty that Muhammad — peace be upon him — reached the highest level of prophethood. You should also make things easier for yourself by adopting his suggestions for religious practices and the effect they have on the purification of hearts. How right he was to say, if a person acts according to what he knows, God will give him knowledge of things which he does not know; "A tyrant's servant will become his slave"; and "If a person devotes all his care to one thing[184] (i.e. the fear of God), God will accept that as payment for (that is, save him from) all the cares of this world and the next." Test these sayings a thousand times, and another thousand times, and you will have acquired a certitude which leaves no room for any doubt.

It is in this way that we seek certainty about prophecy, not by the way of changing a stick into a serpent, or breaking the moon in half.[185] Taken out of context, these could lead to magic, illusion or even a trap set by God, "For He leads astray those that He will, and guides those that He will."[186]

Now one comes to the question of miracles.[187] It may be that you believe in a miracle, basing your belief on a sound argument which proves its existence. It is also possible that your faith in it would be destroyed by another type of reasoning which emphasizes exterior features and the ambiguity of the phenomenon. The example of these unusual actions should be regarded as only one section of your overall reasoning.[188] In this way you will acquire a knowledge that is certain, though you cannot explain its specific basis. This is like someone who acquires information from several different sources and is not able to say precisely which source made him certain. He is certain of the fact, without knowing the precise origin of his certainty; it forms part of a whole, but is not based on this or that statement. That is what we mean by solid and scientific belief.[189] "Personal experience", however, is like "seeing" which consists of "taking by the hand"[190] and can be found only in the mystic way.

What I have said here about the reality of prophecy is sufficient for my present purpose. Now we shall see the great need of the human person for philosophy.

CHAPTER V

THE REASON
WHY I RETURNED TO TEACHING
AFTER HAVING GIVEN IT UP

A. Physicians of the Heart

During my ten years of retreat and solitude it became clear to me from lived experience,[191] by demonstration, or by act of faith that the human person was created with a body and a heart. This heart or spirit is the seat of a person's knowledge of God; it has nothing to do with his flesh and blood, which a corpse or an animal has in common with a human being.

The health of the body makes it happy; illness destroys it. Similarly, the heart can be in good health and nobody shall be saved except one "who comes to God with a pure heart",[192] but on the other hand, the heart can also fall victim to a fatal illness, a "sickness of the heart."[193]

To be ignorant of God is a deadly poison. To disobey Him in order to follow the call of one's own passions causes illness. On the other hand, to know God is the antidote that saves one's life. To obey God, while controlling one's own passions, that is the remedy that restores one's health. As in the case of physical illnesses, it is only by the use of remedies that the illnesses of the heart can be treated and health restored.[194]

Now, the remedies for physical illnesses act by virtue of specific prophecies, which even the brains of intelligent people cannot perceive. Such people have to entrust themselves blindly to physicians who have their science from the prophets. In their capacity as prophets, they know the real quality of things.

In the same way, it became clear to me that it is the same as regards the effectiveness of the practices of worship. Their prescriptions and quantities are defined and measured by the prophets, but what makes them effective cannot be perceived by the intellect. In this case, too, one has to accept the fundamental teaching of the prophets, which they received from the prophetic light, rather than being mediated by the intellect.

Remedies are concocted according to prescribed ratios, e.g.

106

two parts of one substance to one part of another; the secret of this depends on their specific properties. This is also true in the case of religious practices, which are the remedies for the illnesses of the heart. Religious practices consist of many different gestures, in variable proportions. So that two prostrations, *Sujūd,* are equal to one bow, *Rukū,* and a prayer in the afternoon[195] is worth two prayers in the morning. The secret of this is that the particular properties of the practices can only be illuminated by the light of prophecy. One would have to be extremely stupid or extremely ignorant to seek a logical reason for these differences, or to try to explain them by simple coincidence, and not because of a profound divine significance in them which causes them to be such.

On the other hand, every remedy contains a basic substance, to which the medicine is added to create a specific effect.[196] It is the same with prayers or with supererogatory actions:[197] they create the effect when added to the basic elements of the ritual gesture.

To sum up, the prophets are physicians for treating the maladies of hearts. One's brain has no purpose except to enable one to understand this fact. It provides rational assent which supports what the prophets have said, while recognizing its own inability[198] to perceive what the prophetic eye perceives. We are taken by the hand as it were and docilely guided like blind men, or like suffering patients entrusting themselves to their compassionate physicians. That is the limit of our intellect. It has no further purpose beyond enabling the sick person to understand the prescriptions of the physician.[199] That, at least, is what we have gained of necessity from our knowledge, not from our senses, during our years of retreat and solitude.

B. Lukewarm Faith

We have seen how lukewarm is the faith which people have in prophecy, its principles, reality and resulting actions. We have established that this diffident response is due to the actions of four groups: philosophers, mystics, the proponents of teaching and scientists.[200]

I have questioned some of those who try to escape from the divine law, examining their doubts, beliefs and inmost thoughts. I have said to them, "Why do you act to your own disadvantage? It is stupid to sell the Hereafter in exchange for goods of this world. If you believe in the Hereafter but are not preparing to go there yourself, though you would not sell material possessions for half price, you are ready to sell eternity in exchange for the finite number of days you have in this world? On the other hand, if you do not believe in the Hereafter then you are nothing but an infidel! In that case you had better start looking for a religion! If you look for the reason for your secret impiety you can find it in your doctrine buried deep within you.

That is what makes you so bold, although you wish merely to adorn yourself outwardly with an acceptable faith and to profit from the honors paid to the divine law.

One of these men answered me thus: "According to you, the learned should be the first to set a good example. But one of the most famous of them[201] does not perform his prayers; there is another who drinks wine;[202] another devours the assets of religious endowments and the property of orphans; another drains public funds and does not shun forbidden things;[203] finally, there is one who takes bribes to twist his legal decisions and testimony, and so on."

Another claimed that he was so advanced in mysticism that he no longer needed to practice his religion! A third gave the ambiguous excuse of a libertine about freedom.[204] All these have gone astray from the mystic Way.[205]

A fourth person from the company of the proponents of teaching said: "It is difficult to know what is true, for the road to truth is blocked by obstacles. There are many controversies in which one view seems as good as another; rational arguments contradict each other. We cannot trust people's opinions, and those who support teaching state this fact emphatically, without feeling the need to prove its value. In these circumstances is it surprising that we have doubts about what is certain to others?"[206]

A fifth person told me: "I do not act from a simple desire to conform; I have studied philosophy and have perceived the reality of what the prophets said and that it leads to[207] and promotes the public good. The cultic practices they recommend have but one purpose: to bring discipline to the human community, to stop them from killing each other, quarrelling or giving free rein to their passions. But I am not an ignorant nobody who will submit to legal obligations. I am one of the wise and am practiced in wisdom. I see clearly and do not need to practice conformism."

That is the summit of faith for people who have learned philosophy from the theists, and studied the works of Avicenna and Abū Nasr al-Farabi. These are the men who adorn themselves with the trappings of Islam.

It is possible that there are some among them who read the *Qur'ān,* attend assemblies and prayers and pay lip service to the revealed law (*Shari'a*).[208] However, at the same time they continue to drink wine and to behave badly in other ways. If one were to ask them, what is the use of praying, if there is no truth in what the prophets have said? They would doubtless reply, "It is good exercise, it is a local custom, it is a useful system to secure private possessions and family."

It is also possible that they would perceive that the revealed law and that what the prophets said is true. Then should one say: "Why, then, do you drink wine?" Probably they would reply: "Wine is only prohibited because of the excesses which can lead to enmity and hatred. But my wisdom can help me to avoid this; I drink only to sharpen my mind."

Such a person might add that Avicenna wrote that he promised God the Almighty to do such and such things, to promote the revealed law, to practice His religion without negligence, and to drink not for pleasure, but only as a remedy and tonic. Thus, the most that one can demand, both with respect to the faith and to religious practices, would make an exception for wine when taken as a tonic.

That is the belief of people who call themselves believers! Many of them have been led astray by the subjects they have studied, or by the feeble arguments raised against them, which consist merely of rejecting geometry, logic or other exact sciences which are truly necessary for the philosophers, as we have demonstrated above.

C. My Return to Teaching

For all these reasons I perceived that at this point the faith (of all) had become feeble. I felt capable of explaining these errors. I could unmask these fellows more easily than drink a glass of water, because I was completely familiar with the sciences and the ways of the sciences of the mystics, the philosophers, the proponents of

teaching and those who claimed to be learned. My decision suddenly sparked like struck flint, exact and precise: what purpose is
served by solitude and retreat when the sickness is universal, when
the doctors themselves are sick, and humankind is at the point of
perishing?

At that, I began to reflect: "You shall undertake to dissipate
the melancholy and chase away the shadows from this period of
torpor and epoch of error. But you who would wish to bring your
contemporaries back to the right path know well that all will turn
against you. How will you hold your own against them or put up
with them if it is not the propitious moment, and if you do not have
the support of an effective religious authority? It seemed to me that
God was authorizing me to continue my retreat, under the pretext
that I was incapable of successfully arguing the truth."

It was then that, by God the Almighty, the authorities[209] came
to a spontaneous decision, without any outward pressure, and gave
me strict orders to go to Nishāpūr, to fill the vacancy caused by my
absence. The orders were strict enough to put me in danger of being
disgraced if I refused to obey.[210]

It seemed then that my first decision was no longer valid. I
told myself, "You should not choose to remain in solitude just from
laziness and a taste for repose. You do not have the right to wait to
become famous and honored. Nor do you have the right to avoid
contact with other people, for you do not wish to remain in retreat
merely to avoid the difficulties of life in the community."

God has said, "In the name of God the Most Gracious, Most
Merciful. Do men think that they will be allowed to say 'We believe' without being tested? Certainly We have tested their predecessors."[211] God, Mighty and Glorious, also says to His messenger,
the dearest of His creatures, "Certainly, apostles who came before
you have been treated as impostors. They showed fortitude in putt-
ing up with being treated as impostors and abused until they received Our help. No one can escape God's ordinances. Certainly
you have already heard some reports about those We sent."[212]

God, Mighty and Glorious, said also:

In the name of God the most Gracious, most
Merciful, *Yā Sīn*. By the wise *Qur'ān* you are indeed
one of the apostles sent down on a straight path in

order that thou mayest admonish a people whose fathers had received no admonition, and who therefore remain heedless (of the signs of God). The word against the greater part of them is true, for they do not believe. We have put yokes round their necks right up to their chins so that their heads are forced up (and they cannot see). And We have put a bar in front of them and a bar behind them, and further We have blindfolded them, so that they cannot see. It is the same to them, whether thou admonish them or not: they will not believe. You can admonish only one who follows the message.[213]

I then consulted several men of good counsel, men of devotion and visions. They all agreed, telling me to renounce my retreat and to come out of my hiding place.[214] Moreover, righteous men had repeatedly seen dreams about me which foretold good and beneficial effects resulting from my departure. Such was God's will, at the beginning of this sixth century: God — may He be exulted — has indeed promised to revivify His religion at the beginning of each century.[215] All these testimonies gave strength and support to my own hopes.

Finally, thanks to God I departed for Nîshāpūr, in the month of Dhu'l, Qa'da of the year 499 (July, 1106 A.D.). As my departure from Baghdad had been in Dhu'l Qa'da, 488 (November, 1095 A.D.), my retreat lasted eleven years. This change was God's work. I never thought about it in my solitude. It was He who originally inspired me to leave Baghdad and abandon my position. I should not have thought of doing that by myself. It is God the Almighty who changes one's heart and one's situation: "The Gracious one holds the believers's heart between two fingers."[216]

Now I am well aware that, though I seemed to come back to teaching, I did not really do so, because to come back means to return to the previous state. But previously I used to teach in order to obtain honors and to call people to them by my words and deeds. That was my goal and purpose. In contrast, nowadays my teaching invites people to renounce all honors, and shows them how to stop regarding them as important. That is my present intention, goal and desire: in this God is my witness!

I wish to make myself and others better. Whether I shall succeed or die before I achieve my goal I do not know. However, I believe, with a sure faith, based on "sight", that there is no strength or power except in God, the Most High. It was not I who moved, it was He who moved me. It was not I who acted, it was He who made use of me. Therefore, I ask Him, first, to make me better, and then to make other people better by my example; to guide me, then to guide other people through me; to show me the very truth, and grant me to follow it; and to show me absolute wrongdoing, and enable me to avoid it.

D. Remedies for the Lukewarm

Let us return to the causes of tepidity in religion and its remedies in order to deliver the following groups from the causes of their destruction:

1. Those confused by the statements of the proponents of teaching: they should refer to my book, *al-Qisṭās al-Mustaqīm* (The Just Balance), we shall not expand on this text.

2. Those confused by the excuses of the libertines: these are classified into seven categories in our work entitled *Kimyā' al-Sa'ada* (The Alchemy of Happiness).[217]

3. Those whose faith has been destroyed by philosophy, and who reject even the principle of prophecy. I have already spoken about the reality of prophecy and its necessity, basing my argument on the existence of the specific properties of medicines, on knowledge of the stars, and other things as well. The discussion of those matters was only to provide the premise for that argument. I developed this argument precisely because it is drawn from philosophy and I wished to present the proof of prophecy for each separate scientist by drawing on his particular field: astronomy, medicine, the natural sciences, magic, the art of talismans, etc.

4. There are also people who recognize verbal prophecy, but who put the prescriptions of the revealed law on the level of human wisdom, which is really to deny prophecy. Such a person believes only in a sage[218] born under a particular star, for which reason other people follow him; this has nothing to do with prophecy.

Belief in prophecy means certainty regarding the existence of a suprarational zone, where there opens an eye[219] endowed with a particular power of perception. The intellect is excluded from this zone, just as ears cannot perceive colors, eyes cannot perceive sounds, and the senses cannot perceive matters of reason.

Though a friend of the dialecticians may deny the evidence, I have shown the possibility and even its actual existence. If one admits this, one recognizes that there are "properties" which escape understanding or appear almost impossible.

For example, a sixth of a dram[220] of opium is a deadly poison because, due to its excessive cold, it freezes the blood in one's veins. For anyone who calls himself a naturalist bodies cannot be cold except by reason of the two cold elements: earth and water. However it is clear that large quantities of earth and water would not be enough to produce so much cold. Should we say this to a naturalist who has not experimented with this himself, he will say, "It is impossible, because opium contains two other elements, air and fire, and they cannot make anything cold, and even if it were made only of earth and water, it could not freeze anything to such an extent — all the less if it is made of two hot elements." Our expert would think this proved!

Most of the "proofs" brought by the philosophers in natural sciences and in theodicy are of this kind. They represent things to themselves in ways that fit in with their discoveries and the limits of their understanding. Things unfamiliar they declare impossible.

If true dreams[221] were not so common, people who reason like this would refuse to believe that it is possible to discover hidden things while the senses are asleep. If one were to say to one of them, "Is it possible that there exists in this world something only the size of a grain of seed that can destroy a whole town, and then destroy itself entirely?" he would say, "No, that is but fantasy." However, this does happen with fire, in a way that is unbelievable if you have not seen it. Most of the marvels of the other world are like this.[222] To the naturalist we say, "You have to admit that opium has the property of freezing, even if this fact cannot be deduced by logical argument. In the same way, why should prescriptions of the divine law not contain for treating and purifying one's heart properties which cannot be understood by dialectics, but can be perceived by the eye of a prophet?"

Do not the naturalists in their books admit properties which are equally surprising? An example is the use in a difficult birth of the following figure:

4	9	2		D	Ṭ	B
3	5	7		J	H	Z
8	1	6		Ḥ	A	W

The mother-to-be looks at two pieces of cloth which have never been moistened on which this pattern is written. Then she places them under her feet and immediately gives birth. Naturalists mention this case in their tract on "Marvelous properties".[223] The magic pattern consists of nine squares containing nine specific figures which add up to fifteen across, down or diagonally.[224]

How could one believe in this, and not admit that the prescription of two inclinations in morning prayer, four at midday and three at dusk, is because of special properties, unknowable by rational faculties? It is a question of different times of day, whose different properties are perceived only by a prophetic light. Amazingly, if one changed to astrological terms, one would certainly admit these differences in numbering, because the horoscope depends on the position of the sun at noon, at sunrise and at sunset. Upon such things are based the calculations for working out remedies, or determining the length of life and the hour of death.[225] However, there is no difference whatsoever between the zenith and the sun at the equator, or between the west and the setting sun, so how can one believe in astrology? Nevertheless, this false science has its believers, even when they have seen it proven wrong a hundred times! If an astrologer says to them, "When the sun is in the centre of the sky, when such and such a star is turned towards it, and when the ascendant is such and such a sign of the zodiac, if at this moment you are wearing a new outfit you will be killed while wearing it," that would be enough for them never to wear it again, even if they died of cold as a result, and even if the astrologer in question had already lied to them several times!

I would like to know how someone who is sufficiently broad minded to embrace such bizarre beliefs, and must recognize that certain prophets have prodigious properties, can deny what he hears reported of an authentic prophet, a miracle worker who has never lied?

A philosopher denies that such properties are possible as regards the number of *Rakas* (bows in prayer), the ritual throwing of stones,[226] the number of basic elements in a pilgrimage or other religious practices, but they are no different at all from the properties of medicines or of stars.

He might say, "I have experimented myself with certain properties of stars and of medicine and have partly established their existence; therefore I have stopped regarding them with incredulity and mistrust. But, as for prophetic qualities, even if I thought they were possible, how should I know that they existed unless I had personal experience of them?" The answer is this: "Personal experience is not enough, for you always take other people's testimony on trust. Therefore you must trust the words of the prophets: they are speaking from experience and have seen what is true in all that revelation has brought us. You need only follow their path and you will be able to share in their vision of things."

However, I must add, "Even if you did not make this attempt, your common sense would tell you that, in this field, you have to believe and follow blindly." Let us imagine the following case. A reasonable adult who usually is healthy falls ill. His father is a good doctor, as our man has known since he was a child. The father prepares a remedy for his son and tells him, "This is what you need; this will cure you." Though the remedy is bitter, with a dreadful taste, will the patient take it, or will he refuse it, saying, "It is possible that this is the right remedy, but I have not had personal experience of it."

Your doubts make you like this sick person in the eyes of those who can see clearly. If you say, "How shall I know the compassion of the Prophet — peace be upon him — and his knowledge of (spiritual) medicine?" I reply, "How can you know his compassion, which is not apparent to your senses? You can know it in an indubitable manner from the circumstances of his life or the story of his deeds."

Indeed, it is enough to reflect upon the words of God's messenger — peace be upon him — upon the tales of the care which he took to set men upon the right path, upon his generosity towards all creatures, and upon his vigilance in improving their character and relationships, and in making sure that they had everything necessary for this world and the next. It is clear that the Prophet's love for his community surpassed that of a father for his son. Reflect upon the prodigies which he has worked, upon the miracles of the invisible world which have been revealed to the prophet in the *Qur'ān* and which he has told in the traditions, and upon what he foretold about the end of time, which have come to pass as he foretold. It is clear that the prophet crossed the suprarational border, the (third) eye opened for him to reveal the hidden things which only some special persons can see, and to manifest all the things which escape the intellect.

This is what has to be done to be certain of the authenticity of the prophet: try, meditate on the *Qur'ān*, read the traditions and you will see all this with your own eyes.

But this warning to those who side with the philosophers will have to suffice. I have included it, because it seems particularly necessary today.

The fourth cause of lukewarm religion is the sight of the misconduct of scholars. I see three remedies for this:

a. First, this reply: "You see a scholar eating forbidden food. He is as acquainted as are you yourself with wine or usury, slander, lies or calumny. That will not stop you from sinning, but that is from desires, not from lack of faith. The learned man's lust is as strong as yours; it dominates him as much as it does you. The fact that he knows things that you do not know does not increase the degree of prohibition concerning this particular matter.

"How many people believe in medicine, but still eat fruit, or drink cold water, though their doctor has forbidden it! Their imprudent action does not prove that they were right, nor that medicine is worthless. And when wise men behave badly their reasons are not different"

b. A second response is: "The wise man regards his science as his provision for the journey to the Hereafter. He believes that it will save him, that it will intervene in his favor and excuse his bad deeds. The truth is that his knowledge can just as easily turn against him as act in his favor. In any case, he can try to benefit from his science if he has not been a practicing believer. But for you who are not learned, if you make this calculation and neglect religious practices your bad behavior will damn you and there will be nothing to intervene in your favor."

c. Thirdly, a good reply is that a truly learned man does not sin except inadvertently; he does not persevere in error because true knowledge shows him clearly that sin is a deadly poison, and that this world is nothing compared to the Hereafter. Anyone who knows that will not exchange what is of high value for something inferior.

The true knowledge has nothing to do with the other branches of science with which most people busy themselves, and which only lead them to further sins. True knowledge inspires an increase in reverence, awe and hope; it holds people back from sins, except for such as are venial, intermittent and inevitable. These latter do not prove the feebleness of faith, since a believer will succumb and then repent, which is quite different from persevering in error.

That is what I wish to say as a criticism of philosophy and teaching, and in order to reveal the dangers to which a person is exposed if he tries to refute them in inappropriate ways.

We pray God Almighty to count us among the number of those chosen by Him, set by Him upon the right path and led by Him to the truth. May we be among those whom He inspires to call upon Him, so that they do not forget Him; those whom He preserves from their own evil, so that they will love Him alone;[227] and those whom He has made His chosen people, so that they will worship none but Him.

NOTES

1. This is a customary Khuṭba, a brief preface.

2. Specialists on al-Ghazālī agree generally that the addressee is unknown. Probably it is a generic address to all. But I suggest that the addressee is Abū al-Hasan Abdul al-Ghafīr Ibn Isma'il al Fārisī, who met al-Ghazālī and heard from him the experiences about which al-Ghazālī wrote later in *al-Munqidh*. See Ibn Asakir, *Tabyīn Kadhib al-Muftari* (Beirut, Dar al-Kitāb al-Arabi, 1399 A.H./ 1979 A.D.), pp. 294f. (M. Abūlaylah)

3. Not esoteric, but a profound knowledge of Sunnite religious teaching.

4. Concrete truths (*haqq*), rather than truth in general.

5. The term expresses placing a rope on an animal's neck, copying, following blindly and accepting unquestioningly.

6. *Istibsār*: J: observation; W: direct vision; F: assurance; to observe or investigate something hidden; to be able to know by reason, in contrast to conformism; "seeing for oneself".

7. *'Ilm al-Kalām*: Islamic theology; scholastic theology; AGth: defensive apologetic; hence speech about God and His attributes more in´the sense of a defensive apologetic than of "faith seeking understanding", as is often meant by theology in the West.

8. *Al-ta'līm*: teaching, instruction; the authoritative instruction of the infallible Imam, the charismatic leader of the Shi'ites and Bātinites (Interiorists), or other founders of schools of law.

9. Originally, one who presides at prayers; here a combination of religious and political leadership.

10. In the sense of a systematic interpretation of dogma, in some contrast to the modern sense of the term, philosopher. See Majid Fakhry, *A History of Islamic Philosophy* (New York: Columbia University Press, 1970, 2nd ed. 1983).

11. *Taṣawwuf*, those following Sufism as a commitment to a contemplative life; mystical in a broad psychological rather than in a strict technical sense. See Annemarie Schimmel, *Mystical Dimensions of Islam* (Chapel Hill, N.C.: The University of North Carolina Press, 1975).

12. The capital of Khurāsān in northeast Persia.

13. See *Qur'ān* 23:53 and 30:32. It is worth noting that Flügel's edition commonly used in the West has a different numera-

tion of the verses, e.g., the verse 53 of the 1923 Cairo edition mentioned above is numbered 55. (M. Abūlaylah)

14. This *Hadīth* tradition was narrated with some differences as regards its text, in 'Abū Dawūd, al-Termedhī, al-Nasā'ī and Ibn Maja's *Sunan*, via Abū Hurayra. See al-Baghdādī ('Abdu al-Qahir), *al-Farq Bayna al-Firaq* (Beirut: Dar al jil, 1987), pp. 4ff; and N. Rifat, *Dirasat fi Muqarant al-Adyan* (Cairo, 1997), pp. 48ff. (M. Abūlaylah)

15. *Mubtadi'*, one who introduces a *bid'a* or novelty and therefore is considered heterodox by the people of the tradition.

16. One who looks for a deeper, inner, esoteric or allegorical meaning beneath the certitude regarding the revealed teaching. Its meaning as a principle for one's interior life is found only by penetrating to the deep, hidden sense of the dogmatic formulae.

17. See n. 10 above.

18. See n. 7 above.

19. *Zindīq*: free thinker; VR: heretic; BM, F: atheist, from the Persian *Zandikirāy*; *Mu'aṭṭil*: stripping, here regarding the divine attributes.

20. See n. 5 above.

21. The traditions handed down regarding the life and words of the prophet and his companions, as well as the early communities in Macca and Medina.

22. From a root meaning creation, natural disposition; human nature in its original healthy condition.

23. *Qur'ān* 30. 29/30. This is a part of a *Hadīth* reported by Abū Hurayra in Sahih al-Bukhārī. The *Hadīth* in full reads as follows: "No child is born except on *al-fiṭra* (Islam or complete submission) and then his parents make him a Jew, a Christian or a Magian, as an animal produces a perfect young animal: do you see any part of its body deformed." Then he (the prophet) recited: "The religion of pure Islamic faith or pure monotheism is Allah's religion upon which he created mankind, there is no change in Allah's religion, that is indeed the right religion" (al-Bukhārī, *Kitāb al-Tafsīr*, no. 298). (M. Abūlaylah)

24. Note that al-Ghazālī is not rejecting all *Taqlidāt* or traditional beliefs. Here he is about to examine the crisis of skepticism, in contrast to his own later and much deeper crisis of conscience or spirit. (See our translation of this highly valuable book, *Kitāb al-*

'Ilm. M. Abūlaylah.)

25. This definition of sure and certain knowledge (*al-'ilm al-yaqīnī*) is a basic premise for what follows. McCarthy in his n. 27 compares it to the *mutakallimūn*'s necessary knowledge, namely, knowledge that imposes such compulsion that one cannot escape it or retain any doubt or suspicion about it.

26. *Al-qawl fī madākhil al-safsata wa jahd al-'ulūm.* J: The sophists and the radical problem of knowledge; W: skepticism and the denial of all knowledge.

27. *Al-Ḥissiyyāt.*

28. *Al-ḍarūriyyāt*: things necessary in the sense of n. 25 above; self-evident in the sense of analytic propositions which when understood must be accepted, or metaphysical propositions entailed by the judgment of being.

29. The objects of *taqlīd* as unquestioning conformism to authority.

30. *Al-Naẓariyyāt*: related to speculation or reasoning.

31. These are examples of his meaning of primary or basic truths, *awwaliyyāt*.

32. Al-Ghazālī mistakenly considered the text in quotation marks as a *Ḥadīth* (prophetic saying). Abū Bakr Ibn al-Arabī stated that it is a part of a speech (*Khuṭba*) and not a *Ḥadīth* at all (al-'Awasim min al-Qawasim, vol. 2, pp. 16f); Muḥammad al-Ḥūt, refers this saying back to Imām Ali-Ibn Abū Ṭālib. See Asma al-Matalib fī Ahadith Mukhtalifat al-Maratib, referred to in the Saliba and 'Ayyād edition of *al-Munqidh*, p. 86 fn. 1. (M. Abūlaylah)

33. *Qur'ān* 50.21/22.

34. McCarthy sees this as a real but passing crisis of skepticism in one's early teens, common to young reflective persons in the first flush of self-assertion as they face adulthood. He distinguishes this from the greater crisis to come. V. Poggi, *Un Classico della Spiritualità Musulmana* (Roma: Gregoriana, 1967), p. 171ff, considers the youthful crisis to be one of methodological, rather than real, skepticism. In any case, al-Ghazālī is clear that he was not a philosophical skeptic, a heretic or a real unbeliever. See introduction.

35. As a convinced occasionalist, for al-Ghazālī there was only one agent. Here breast refers especially to the heart (*qalb*) taken as the seat of the intelligence and closely related to soul

(*nafs*), spirit (*rūh*) and reason or intellect (*'aql*). (See al-Ghazālī, *Ihyā''Ulūm ad-Dīn* [*Revivification of the Religious Sciences*] [Cairo: Istiqāmā, 1352/1933]), Book XXI. "Light" would appear to apply primarily to intelligence. His statement that this is "cast" by God into his breast should be understood at least in terms of occasionalism as a common act of God, or more probably in terms of faith as a special grace.

36. *Kashf,* unveiling of truth; by this expression al-Ghazālī means to clear away the doubts which surround real knowledge of things. By letting light fall on them they are clear as daylight. This is made possible by the light which illumines the heart. This light is like a mirror which enables one to see clearly everything that falls on it as long as there are no impurities in it (*Ihyā'*, vol. 1, p. 31). *Mukāshafa* according to al-Hujwīrī (4th-5th century A.H.) denotes the presence of the Spirit (*Sirr*) in the domain of actual vision (*'Ayān*). *Kashf al-Mahjūb*, translated by Nicholson (Delhi: Taj Company, 1989), p. 373. (M. Abūlaylah)

37. *Qur'ān*, 6/125.

38. This *Hadīth* is reported by Ibn Abū al-Duniyya, in *Qisaral-Amal*, al-Hākim in *al-Mustadrak*, Ibn Jarīr and Ibn Kathīr in their Tafsīr. (M. Abūlaylah)

39. This *Hadīth* is reported by Ahmad in *al-Musnad*, by al-Tirmidhī, al-Tabarani and al-Hakim through Abdul Allah Ibn Umar. (M. Abūlaylah)

40. This *Hadīth* is reported with different wording by Ibn al-Najjār who took it from Ibn Umar, al-Bayhaqī Sunan, Abū Nu'aim, Hilya, and al-Hakim via Anas. (M. Abūlaylah)

41. *Ahl al-Hadra, al-Hudūr* or *al-Muhādara* is a Sufi term denoting the presence of the heart in the subtleties of demonstration (*bayān*), while the *Mukāshafa* denotes the presence of the Spirit (*Sirr*) in the domain of actual vision (*'Ayān*). In *Kashf al-Mahjūb* al-Hujwīrī states that *Muhadara* refers to the proofs of God's signs, *Ayāt* and *Mukāshafa* to the proofs of contemplation or reflection upon God's creation (p. 373). (M. Abūlaylah)

42. See al-Ghazālī's statement about 'Ibn al-Kalām in *Ihyā' Ulūm al-Dīn* (Beirut: al-Kutub al-Ilmiyya, 1412 A.H./1992 A.D.), vol. 1, pp. 52f. I have already translated al-Ghazālī's book of knowledge, which is in preparation. (M. Abūlaylah)

43. *Al-akhbār*: news, reports; often used for *Hadīth* or the ac-

counts of the sayings and actions of the Prophet Muḥammad.

44. *Sunnah*: etymologically, custom, path, way or traditional rules of conduct; juridically the *Ḥadīth*, or verbal, actual and tacit teaching of the Prophet, and the established practice of the community.

45. *Kalām*: is described by Ibn Khaldūn (AGth 121-24) as containing both rational proofs of the articles of faith and refutations of the innovators. Al-Ghazālī saw the need for such competency in each community, but considered it less important than *fiqh* or jurisprudence which engages daily life. Al-Ghazālī had studied *kalām* at a rather early age under the Imām al-Ḥaramayn.

46. He criticizes both a too ready acceptance of the *ijmā* or consensus and a non-critical acceptance of a supposed meaning of a tradition or text.

47. The sickness of skepticism. Though described above as cured in his own life, in this part he is proceeding systematically, rather than chronologically, to describe the ways of acquiring sure knowledge.

48. The sections on epistemology and ontology are more developed in the later manuals of *kalām*.

49. Jabre has only the title without this descriptive paragraph, which is found in McDonald.

50. Al-Ghazālī was first of all an expert in religious law (*fiqh*), which was the main subject at the Niẓāmiyya school.

51. *Takhyīl*: J: imaginary; F: illusion; W: delusions; BM: fictions.

52. *Al-kufr wal'ilḥād*: *kufr* or unbelief excludes the unbeliever from the community of believers. *Ilḥād*: deviating from the true religion; also atheism or godlessness.

53. *Al-dahriyyūn*: materialists, from *dahr* or endless time and blind fate.

The *Qur'ān* referred to the *dahriyyūn* and their belief and character in the following verse:

"Hast thou seen him who has taken his caprice to be his God, and God has led him astray out of a knowledge, and set a seal upon his hearing and his heart, and laid a covering on his eyes? Who shall guide him after God? What will you not remember? They say, There is nothing but our present life, we die, and we live, and nothing but time destroys us. Of that they have no knowledge. They merely conjecture (*Qur'ān*: 45: 24f). In this way Allah reveals the corrupt nature of the materialists and their baseless belief." (Ibn Manẓūr *Lisān al-'Arab.* Vol. 4, p. 293.) (M. Abūlaylah)

54. With the exception of al-Kindī the Islamic philosophers held that the world was eternal, emanating from the One or First after the fashion of Neo-Platonic thought. Here al-Ghazālī is referring to the pre-Socratic philosophers.

55. Emphatic plural of *zindīq*: godless in the fullest sense of the term. (*Lisān al-'Arab.* Vol. 10, p. 147.)

56. *Al-Ṭabī'iyyūn*: naturalists, from *ṭabī'a* or nature; also "element". (al Mu'jam al-Falsafi Majma al-Lughat al'Arabiyya.)

57. The argument from design for the existence of God.

58. *I'tidāl al-mizāj*: *mizāj*, mixture or combination of hot, cold, moist and dry, whose combination since ancient times was held to determine the physiological quality of a body. (*al-Mu'jam al-Falsafi*, 189. Cairo, 1983, p. 177.)

59. In Islamic eschatology since the *Qur'ān*, "Garden" and "Fire" refer to Heaven and Hell; the "Assembly", "Recall", and "Resurrection" (*al-ḥashr wa 'l-nashr wa 'l-qiyāma*) refer to the resurrection on the last day; "Reckoning" is the Judgment on the Last Day.

60. From *ilāh* or God; Allāh (God) is a contraction of *al-ilāh* (*The God*). (See al-Mu'jam al-Falsafi, p. 179.)

61. *Qur'ān*, 33.25. "God spared the believers from fighting (the unbelievers)," which traditionally is explained as being due to the infighting of the unbelievers.

62. Ibn Sīnā, commonly referred to as *al Shaykh al-Ra'īs* (the master of masters); born 370/980 near Bukhārı; died in 428/1037 in Hamadān; an Aristotelian with a strong neo-Platonic influence.

63. Often called "The Second Teacher," Aristotle being the First; born about 870, died at Damascus in 339/950; principally a commentator on Aristotle.

64. For example, *al-Kindī* and *al-Rāzī* (*Rhazes*).

65. To accept what is worthy of being termed unbelief (*Takfīr*) would render one *Kufr*, excommunicate one from the community of believers, and make one subject to formal judgment whose punishment is death. To accept what is termed innovation (*bida'h*), that is, something not conformed to the *Salaf* or ancients who guard the Tradition, would make one a heretic but not a non-

Muslim.

66. *Umūr burhāniyya*, the result of apodeictic demonstration (*burhān*).

67. *Ta'tīlihim*, their denial of divine attributes.

68. *Al-awā'il*: the ancient philosophers.

69. *Shahwatu'l-bātala*, rather than *al-shahwatu 'l-bātila* (vain passion).

70. The ancient philosophers considered mathematics a propedeutic to philosophy; al-Kindī makes it an essential precondition.

71. *Al-Shar'*: revealed law.

72. *ta'arrud*: undertakes; W: opposed.

73. Tradition. It is told that a year before his death the Prophet lost a son Ibrāhīm, by Mary the Copt, on the day of an eclipse and that Muhammad wanted to put an end to the supposition of many that the two were related. This *Hadīth* appears in *al-Jāmi' al-Saghīr* with little difference in wording. (M. Abūlaylah)

74. *'Ilm al-hisāb*: W: the science of arithmatic; F: astronomical calculation.

75. I.e., it is not in one of the six sound collections of the *Hadīth* tradition. (M. Abūlaylah)

76. *Tasawwur*: concept; *tasdīq*: assent or judgement, but here not a judgment of evidence. For Ibn Sīnā *tasdīq* signifies assent or adherence to a judgement.

77. *Ahl al-nazar*: those engaged in speculation, e.g., the Mu'tazilites, Ash'arites' and some in jurisprudence.

78. If *ilayhi* is taken to refer to students of logic, the "too" adds the student of mathematics; W: unbelief; F: logic.

79. *Tahāfut*: incoherence, collapse, inconsistency; the translation used in the Middle Ages was "destructio"; completed in 488/1095. The translation of *Tahāfut al-Falāsifah* into English is by Michael E. Marmura *Al-Ghazalī, The Incoherence of the Philosophers* (Provo, Utah: Brigham Young University Press, 1997).

This translation is perfectly good and of great help for the students of al-Ghazālī world wide. It appears in a parallal English-Arabic text with valuable introduction and annotation. (M. Abūlaylah)

80. Al-Ghazālī implies *Qur'ān* 7:54 "Surely your Lord is God, who created the heavens and the earth in six days, then sat Himself upon the throne, covering the day with the night it pursues

urgently, and the sun, and the moon and the stars subservient, by His command."

"It is Allah who created the heavens and the earth, and sent down out of heaven water wherewith He brought forth fruits to be your sustenance. And He subjected to you the ships to run upon the sea at His commandment; and He subjected to you the rivers and He subjected to you the sun and the moon constant upon their courses, and He subjected to you the night and day, and gave you of all you asked Him . . ." (14:34).

"It behooves not the sun to overtake the moon, neither does the night outstrip the day, each swimming in a sky . . . ." (36:40)

81. It is perhaps worth listing these twenty headings, as given by al-Ghazālī in the *Tahāfut*, since the reader may not have easy access to Kemali or VDB. They are as follows:

1) The refutation of their doctrine on the pre-eternity (*azaliyya*) of the world.

2) The refutation of their doctrine on the post-eternity (*abadiyya*) of the world.

3) Exposé of their deception in their affirming that God is the Maker of the world, and that the world is of His making.

4) On showing their inability to prove the existence of the Maker.

5) On showing their inability to establish proof of the impossibility of (the existence of) two Gods (i.e. to prove the unity of God).

6) On the refutation of their doctrines on the denial of (God's) Attributes.

7) On the refutation of their affirmation that the essence of the First is not divisible into genus and specific difference.

8) On the refutation of their affirmation that the First is a simple being without a quiddity.

9) On showing their powerlessness to demonstrate that the First is not a body.

10) On showing that they are logically bound to hold the eternal existence of the world (*dahr*) and to deny the existence of the Maker.

11) On showing their inability to affirm that the First knows anything other than Himself.

12) On showing their inability to affirm that he knows Himself.

13) On the refutation of their affirmation that the First does not know particulars.

14) On their affirmation that the heaven is an animal (*haya-wān*: living being) which moves voluntarily.

15) On the refutation of what they mentioned of the aim (purpose) which moves heaven.

16) On the refutation of their affirmation that the souls of the heavens know all the particulars.

17) On the refutation of their affirmation of the impossibility of violation of customs (*kharq al-'ādāt*).

18) On their affirmation that the soul of man is a substance subsisting in itself and neither a body nor an accident.

19) On their affirmation of the impossibility of ceasing-to-be (annihilation) for human souls.

20) On the refutation of their denial of the resurrection of bodies with consequent pleasure and pain in the Garden and the Fire by reason of bodily pleasures and pains.

82. *Tuḥshar*: assembled, the resurrection of man's bodies on the Last Day. The key Islamic philosophers so interpreted this that it lost its literal meaning.

83. *Qur'ān*, 34.3. The difficulty lies in reconciling God's omniscience and His immutability. God knows everything, but without change in His knowledge as would be the case were He to know an event first as future, then as present and finally as past.

84. This involves the issue of the creation of the world from nothing as regards itself.

85. McCarthy would see this phrase as applying to all three points as well as to any one of them separately. Though critical of those who would easily accuse others of heresy, al-Ghazālī does not hesitate to say that no one who affirmed any one of these could be truly Muslim.

86. Mu'tazilites reflect the *kalām* in its primitive form. Their doctrine is marked by the following positions: (a) a great sinner is neither an infidel nor a believer, but between the two; (b) one is responsible for his or her actions due to free will; (c) the absolute unity of God, with no distinction of Essence and Attributes; (d) the

ability of reason to distinguish good and evil. They gave importance to Greek philosophy.

87. Appendix I in R. McCarthy, *Freedom and Fulfillment* (Boston: Twayne, 1980), pp. 145-174.

88. *Al-anbiyā'*: J: the predecessors of the prophet; or *al-awliyā'*: W: the saints of old.

89. McCarthy would trace their ethics also to Greek sources. Al-Ghazālī's own work *Mīzān al-'amal* reflects other sources.

90. *Dhikr Allāh*: *dhikr*, remembrance, invoking; namely, the Sufi practice of repeating the name of God or certain formulas or verses.

91. *Awtād al-ard*: literally means *watad*, tent peg or pole; in the plural a group of Saints headed by the *qutb* (pole or pivot), or the saint in each age who supports and directs the world. The expression *Awtād al-ard*, as used by al-Ghazālī, goes back to Imām Ali Ibn Abi Tálib, the prophet's son in law and cousin (Beirut: *Nahj al-Balāgha*, vol. 1, pp. 151, 153). (M. Abūlaylah)

92. See *Qur'ān*, Sura XVIII, related to the seven sleepers of Ephesus.

93. The fourth orthodox Caliph (656-661), husband of Fatimā, assassinated at Kūfa. He is at the source of the scism which divided Moslems into Shī'ites and Sunnis.

94. *Al-qallāb*: W: counterfeiter; McCarthy: a "confidence man" who handles counterfeit money, but does not actually produce it.

95. Ikhwān al-Safā: mid-fourth century at Basra, with religious, philosophical and political interests of Mu'tazilite, Ismā'īlite and Karramite tendencies.

96. *al-mustaqdhar*: deemed impure in a legal sense.

97. *Ta'lim*: teaching. *Ta'limism* is the last form of Shī'ite Isma'ilism. All things have an apparent (*Zāhir*) and a hidden (*Bātin*) aspect which can be perceived only under the direction of an infallible teacher. Hence al-Ghazālī refers to it also as *bātinism*.

98. *Mā fī kinānatihim*: what is in their quiver, that is, what is the strength of their position.

99. *Fadā'ih al-Bātiniyya wa Fadā'il al-Mustazhiriyya (The Infamies of the Bātinites and the Virtues of Mustazhirites)* written in 487/1094-1095. See McCarthy, Appendix II.

100. Sunnite ash'arites, followers of Al-Ash'ri and called "*ahl*

al Ḥaqq".

101. Aḥmad Ibn Ḥanbal was born in Baghdad 164/780-241/855, a champion of rigid literal orthodoxy of the traditionalist Hanbalite school of *fiqh* and defender of the eternity of the *Qur'ān*.

102. Al-Ḥārith al-Muḥāsibī was born in Baghdad 243/857, ascetic and jurist in the shāfi'ite school of *fiqh*.

103. *Qur'ān* 5:3.

104. *Al-ijtihād wa l-ra'y: ijtihād*, effort, a legal term for the personal effort made to answer a question whose answer is not clear from the *Qur'ān* or tradition. *Ra'y:* individual reasoning, was originally practically synonymous with *ijtihād*.

105. The Batinite Ta'limites rejected reasoning as a source of certitude in order to reinforce the need for a teacher.

106. Mu'adh Ibn Jabal cited three steps: first, the *Qur'ān* if it had relevant texts; second, the *sunna* or custom of the Prophet; lacking both he would use personal judgment. This *Hadīth* appears also in this form in al-Ghazālī's book *al-Mankhūl*, p. 331. It is narrated by Ahmad, Abū Dāwūd and al-Tirmidhī. But al-Bukhārī does not consider it a sound *Hadīth* according to his own measure. Al-Tirmidhī says also it lacks the uninterrupted chain of authority (see Ibn al-Athīr al-Jazarī, *Jāmi' al'-Uṣūl fī Ahādīth al-Rasūl*, edited by A. al-Arna'ūt (Beirut, Dar al-Fikr, 1403 A.H./1933 A.D.), vol. 10, pp. 178-179. (M. Abūlaylah)

107. The direction of Macca toward which one should turn in prayer.

108. "Legal alms", the obligation of the *zakāt*, one of the five pillars of Islam.

109. 80/696-150/767, one of the four great teachers of law whose system is still the most followed. He accepted reason (*ra'y*) and analogical reason in interpreting revelation and judicial sentences, corrected by personal assessment (*istihsān*) of present circumstances.

110. Ghazza 150/767-Fustāt 204/820. Also among the four greats, he accepted general consensus, but rejected *ra'y* and *istihsān*.

111. Schools of *fiqh*.

112. This saying is not to be found in any of the *Hadīth* collections. Al-Irāqī and al-Muzanī both declared it inauthentic. (M. Abūlaylah)

113. *Qawā'id al-'aqā'id*, the title of Book II of al-Ghazālī's

ʾā

114. *Al-Qisṭās al-Mustaqīm*, a work in logic.

115. The five balances are the five forms of the syllogism. Al-Ghazālī learned them from the logicians, but could illustrate them from the *Qur'ān*.

116. The Fatimid Caliph, Egypt.

117. By this statement al-Ghazālī indirectly refers to the theory of Takafú al-Adilla, equivalence of evidences. (M. Abūlaylah)

118. *Mansus 'alayhi*: *naṣṣ*, a text in which the prophet explicitly designated it, in contrast to *ikhtiyār*, choice or election as with the Sunnites.

119. Al-Ghazālī manifests a minimist apologetic attitude, but does not attempt to ground theology in subjective experience rather than objective revelation.

120. The problem of *Iḍlāl* (leading astray) arises from the *Qur'ān* 16.95/93. "He leads astray whom He will." Al-Ghazālī is a strong predestinarian.

121. Still a popular proverb in Baghdad. The phrase *Fakhburhum Taqlu-hum*, goes back to Imām Ali Ibn Abi Tālib. Some authorities referred it back to the prophet Muḥammad. But there is evidence to support the opinion first mentioned. (See Nahju l-Balāgha, vol. 4, p. 101.) (M. Abūlaylah)

122. *Tarīqa*: method, road or way (generally capitalized) to indicate a particular way, or a Sufi "order".

123. *A'mālihim*: works or practice according to Watt, Veccia and Rubinacci; McCarthy has *'ilmihim*, knowledge.

124. *Nafs* as reflexive, its etymological sense.

125. Died in Baghdad, 386/996; head of the Sālimiyya theological system of Basra.

126. See n. 92 above.

127. Died in 289/920. See Schimmel, pp. 57-79.

128. Baghdad 247/861-334/945. See Schimmel, pp. 77-80.

129. Died 261/875 or 264/887. See Schimmel, pp. 47-51.

130. *Al-dhawq*: J: taste or tasting, synonymous with *Idrāk* or direct knowledge, in contrast to knowledge through a middle term; knowledge not only as insight, but also as enjoyment and intoxication. This is higher than both *taqlīd*: faith based on conformism, and *'ilm*: knowledge. For W it is: immediate experience accompanied by savoring.

131. *al-ḥāl*: state, condition; a mystic ecstatic state in Sufi writings.

132. *Tabaddul al sifāt*: change of qualities in the sense of a moral change consisting in acquiring virtues; this is to put on the moral qualities of God, and His attributes and Names.

133. *Wa mā ma'ahu min al-ṣahwi* (sobriety); can be read as parallel to *wa mā ma'ahu min al-sukri shay'*.

134. *W: al-sāhi*: a sober person; in Abūlaylah's Arabic text and *M: Wa al-ṭabīb*: the physician which is more coherent to the text.

135. Many Sufis refused to write on their experiences which they considered ineffable.

136. Al-Hujwīrī says that the way to Allah consists of three kinds:

(1) *Maqām*, is a technical Sufi term meaning the perseverance of the traveler in the way of Allah in fulfilling his obligations towards the object of his search with persuasion and flawless intention. Maqam is the beginning of man's search for Allah.

(2) *Ḥāl*, is an attribute of the object desired (*Murād*), while *waqt*, time, is the rank of the desirer (*Murīd*). Ḥāl adorns time as the Spirit adorns the body.

(3) *Tāmkīn*, firmness; it denotes the firm stay of spiritual adepts in the abode of perfection and at the highest grade. (See *Kashf al-Mahjūb*, pp. 368ff.) (M. Abūlaylah)

137. Al-Ghazālī was firmly committed to these three principles or fundamentals, even during his earlier epistemological crisis. Now he begins his account of his religious spiritual crisis regarding being wholly committed to the way which follows logically upon these three fundamental principles.

138. He had been teaching *fiqh*, which he still considered to be of value, even in contrast to *kalām* and medicine.

139. *Takhyīl*: fakery, make-believe; F: fantasy.

140. McCarthy considers fear of assassination by the Bātinites not to be the major factor here. He reads these paragraphs as a moving account of a classic personal religious crisis, ending in a true conversion. "He received divine grace which was at once a call and a help to personal holiness; he accepted the grace and really became a holy man." McCarthy p. 134, n. 172.

141. *Qur'ān* 27. 63/62.

142. *Qur'ān* 53. 31/30.

143. *Samāwī*: heavenly, preternatural, abnormal.

144. The Umayyad Mosque, whose minaret is now called the Minaret of al-Ghazālī.

145. Believed to be the place whence Muḥammad — (Peace be upon Him) — began his *Mi'rāj* or ascension to the seven heavens.

146. *al-khalīl*: Abraham — the tomb in Hebron.

147. In Arabia the holy cities of Macca, birthplace of Muḥammad (Peace be upon Him), where the Ka'ba is visited; and Madina to which Muḥammad (Peace be upon Him) emigrated (Higra, 662 A.D.) to organize Islam. Muḥammad's tomb is visited there.

148. 488/1095-499/1105.

149. An allusion to the Sūrat al-Nūr. See *Qur'ān* 24.35: "God is the light of the heaven and the earth; the likeness of His light is a niche wherein is a lamp." Al-Ghazālī wrote *The Niche of Lights* (Mishkāt al-Anwār) trans. W.H.T. Gairdner (London, 1924).

150. *Takbīrat-al-iḥrām*: the opening formula for prayer: *Allāhu akbar*: God is Greater (than all else).

151. *al-fanā'*: annihilation.

152. "To it", i.e., to *al-fanā* i.e, annihilation; though Sihimel and Barbier de Meynard consider "it" to refer to the Way.

153. *Al-ḥulūl*: dismounting, taking up residence; J and W: inherence; McCarthy: in-dwelling, fusion.

154. *al-ittiḥād*: J and W: union, F: identification.

155. *Al-wuṣūl*: J: connection; F and BM: intimate union.

156. By the poet, Ibn al-Mu'tazz (d. 908 A.D.).

157. *Karāmāt al'awliyā'*: in the orthodox view there is no difference between these states and *mu'jizāt*, the miracles by which the prophet gave signs of the truth of the prophecy, though this was not held by the Mu'tazalites.

158. *Awliyā'*: friends, close associates; here, close to God.

159. Outside of Macca.

160. *'Ashiq*: to love passionately, in contrast to *aḥabbā*, simply to love.

161. *Yashqā*: wretched.

162. Book XXI, the first book of the third quarter of the *Iḥya'*.

163. *'ilm*: apodictic knowledge.

164. *dhawq*, taste, means spiritual delight. It should be noted that *dhawq* resembles *Shurb* (drinking), but the latter is used solely in reference to pleasure, whereas the former is applied to pleasure and pain alike. (See *Kashf al-Mahjūb*, pp. 58, 392.) (M. Abūlaylah)

165. *Imān*: here probably not religious faith in God, but trust in human testimony. The word can mean both.

166. *Qur'ān* 58.11. There was a hierarchy of places in the Council of the Prophet and in other meetings according to those who believe and those to whom knowledge is given. The hierarchy here could be either ascending with primacy given to faith, or descending of kinds of knowledge (ma'rifa).

167. *Qur'ān*, 47.18/16.

168. *Ḥaqīqa*: the reality and special character of prophecy. "Necessary" suggests a very close similarity between the knowledge of the Sufi and that of the Prophet. (Kashf al-Mahjub, p. 382). (M. Abūlaylah)

169. *Fī aṣl al-fiṭra*: in his original condition. *Fiṭra*: creation, natural disposition or constitution.

170. *Qur'ān*, 74.31.

171. *Yanfukhu fīhi*: there is breathed into him; *yanfatih*: M: there is opened.

172. *Al-aswāt wa l-naghamāt*: M: voices and melodies; J: sounds and melodies; F: the sense of hearing succeeds.

173. *Al-wājibāt*: the necessary; *al-jā'izāt*: the possible; *al-mustahīlāt*: the impossible.

174. *Nubuwwa*: prophecy, prophethood, described as "another eye" or kind of vision superior to the normal intellection. Some Islamic philosophers relate this to the active intellect. Jabre considers this not a suprarational faculty, but the full development of the intellect. Watt differs on this in "The Authenticity of Works Attributed to al-Ghazālī," *JRAS* (1952), 26-27.

175. *Al-nawm*: sleeping. Here al-Ghazālī is referring to dreaming.

176. Just as the eye cannot see without light, the eye of the prophet needs a special "light". Many Islamic philosophers speak of a reception of "species" or impressions from the active intellect.

177. Al-Ghazālī's argument on the possibility of prophecy is based not on a theoretical analysis of its nature, but simply on the

fact that similar knowledge does exist.

178. This property of prophecy, perception of things not ordinarily perceptible to the intellect, is but one of its properties; others are perceptible only to one who follows the Way of Sufism.

179. Experience not only in the objective sense, but also in the more ample subjective sense of being lived, tasted and enjoyed (see n. 118 above).

180. Here the main point is that knowledge obtained through prophecy is of the same nature as that had through the practice of Sufism.

181. *Li mushāhadati ahwālihim*: seeing them do their work.

182. Founder of a school of *fiqh*. See note 100 above.

183. He had great influence on Arab medicine.

184. A single care, that is, about God and the things of God; literally: whoever makes all his cares a single care.

185. The stick is that of Moses (see *Qur'ān* 20.72-73/69-70; 26.44/45). Splitting the moon is said of Muhammad based on *Qur'ān* 54.1. The problem here concerns prophecy, not a philosophy of knowledge in general.

186. *Qur'ān* 16.93.

187. *Wa taridu 'alayaka as'ilat al-mu'jizāt* ("Now then the questions concerning miracles will come to your mind"). If placed at the end of the preceding paragraph it gives the sense that if one justifies belief in prophecy by apologetic principles then one is faced with all the issues relating to miracles.

188. McCarthy and Poggi argue against MacDonald and van Leeuwen, that an historical agnosticism about miracles is not implied by al-Ghazālī's position that they are proven rather through the person of the prophet. Rather, this is a balanced position rooting personal conviction in objectively revealed data, as seen in the above paragraph regarding doubt concerning the divine inspiration of a particular prophet.

189. *Fa hādha huwa l-īmān al-qawiyy al-ilmiyy*: this then is strong belief based on knowledge; W: strong intellectual faith; F: the characteristics of scientific certitude. Note a certain ambiguity as to *īmān* and *'ilmī*.

190. See below, Va.

191. See n. 188 above.

192. *Qur'ān*, 26.89.

193. *Qur'ān*, 2.9/10.

194. McCarthy suggests: remedies are the only way to treat the heart by removing its malady and securing its health. He suggests that reading *li 'izālatihi* for *bi 'izālatihi* would remove the ambiguity of the text.

195. McCarthy has *salāt al-ẓuhr*: noon prayer. The *salāt al-subh* has two *rak'as* (series of formulas and postures) whereas the *salāt al-zhur* and the *salāt al-'asr* have four *rak'as*.

196. *'Amāl* can be read either as *a'māl*: workings, actions; or as *i'māl*: activation, making work.

197. *Al-sunan*: customs or usages, especially of the Prophet; here something recommended and meritorious. *Nawāfila*: supererogatory works or prayers.

198. *Bil-'ajz*: J: inability, or M: *bil-'amā*: blindness.

199. *Yulqīhī*: lays down, proposes. Note the limitations al-Ghazālī conceived for the role of reason.

200. The four major divisions of seekers of truth are listed here in terms of their religious attitudes. The fourth class is characterized by the possession of knowledge; *al-mawsūmīn bi l-'ilm*, i.e., the *'ulamā* (theologians) and *fuqahā* (jurisprudents).

201. *al-fuḍalā'*: plural of eminent, outstanding, learned.

202. *al-khamar*.

203. *al-Harām*: legally forbidden.

204. Ibāha: a sect which separated from the Sufis; *ahl al-ibāha*: men of permissiveness, licentiousness.

205. *'an al-tasawwuf*: have gone astray through a misuse of Sufism.

206. *Mutahakkim*: to make categorical pronouncements, and to do so arbitrarily (*lā hujjata Lahu*) as needing no proof. That is, as the Ta'līmite alone possesses the truth, his certainties are not to be given up (*ada'u*) for the uncertainties of others.

207. This was not properly wisdom or philosophy, but an empirical ethic based on knowledge of God and seen as a kind of technique with its own laws and object.

208. The revealed law.

209. Fakhr al-Mulk, minister of Sanjār.

210. *Ilā-hadd al-wahsha*: in my disgrace (loneliness, estrangement).

211. *Qur'ān*, 29.1-2.

212. *Qur'ān*, 6.34.

213. *Qur'ān*, 36.1-10/1-11. Apostles must expect opposition and trials but must continue with their work, even when there seems to be no result.

214. *Zāwiya.*

215. According to Ibn 'Asākir the reformers are: first century: 'Umar; Second century: al-Shāfi'i; third century: al-Asha'rī; fourth century: al-Baqillānī; and fifth century: al-Ghazālī.

216. Al-Ghazālī explains the two fingers as an angel and a devil; the heart is changed according as it follows the suggestions of one or the other.

217. See H.A. Homes, translation from the Turkish (Albany, N.Y.: Munsell, 1873); C. Field's translation from the Hindu has only six categories.

218. See n. 193 above.

219. See n. 160 above.

220. *Dāniq*: two carats, an ancient coin; *drachme* (*dirham*): an eighth of an ounce.

221. *Ru'yā*: ordinary dream, considered to be the 46th part of prophecy.

222. The rejection of the strange features of the world-to-come usually belongs to this class. This can refer as well to anything beyond ordinary experience, especially the object of the "eye" of prophecy.

223. *fi'ajā'ibi l-khawāss.* J, W and VR consider this to be a special book, whereas Sch and BM do not.

224. The *Jadwal*, "the Threefold talisman of al-Ghazālī" to invoke God's help. I. Lichtenstadter suggests that the number 15 reflects the Jewish practice of avoiding the letters which compose the name *Yahweh*: *yōdh* and *hē*, which for both Arab and Jew carry the value of 10 and 5 respectively.

225. *al-a'mār wa l-ajāl*: one's appointed time of death was discussed theologically in relation to divine providence and human freedom.

226. Before entering the Ka'ba; one of the practices of the pilgrimage (*hajj*) which in turn is one of the five pillars of Islam.

227. *Qur'ān*, 12.54.

INDEX

G

H

www.ingramcontent.com/pod-product-compliance
Lightning Source LLC
Chambersburg PA
CBHW061538120726

48001CB00004B/1606